YONDER COME DAY

Exploring the Collective Witness of the Formerly Enslaved

JASMINE L. HOLMES

BakerBooks
a division of Baker Publishing Group
Grand Rapids, Michigan

Published by Baker Books
a division of Baker Publishing Group
Grand Rapids, Michigan
BakerBooks.com

Printed in the United States of America

Library of Congress Cataloging-in-Publication Data
Names: Holmes, Jasmine L., 1990– author.
Title: Yonder come day : exploring the collective witness of the formerly enslaved / Jasmine L. Holmes
Description: Grand Rapids, Michigan : Baker Books, a division of Baker Publishing Group, [2024] | Includes bibliographical references.
Identifiers: LCCN 2024005422 | ISBN 9781540904515 (casebound on demand) | ISBN 9781540903174 (paperback) | ISBN 9781493447039 (ebook)
Subjects: LCSH: Enslaved persons—United States—Interviews. | Enslaved persons—Religious life—United States. | Slave narratives—United States. | Slavery—United States—History. | Federal Writers' Project.
Classification: LCC E444 .H655 2024 | DDC 306.3/62092273—dc23/eng/20240324
LC record available at https://lccn.loc.gov/2024005422

Scripture is taken from the King James Version of the Bible.

Cover design by Lauren Smith.

The author is represented by the literary agency of The Gates Group, www.the-gates-group.com.

Baker Publishing Group publications use paper produced from sustainable forestry practices and postconsumer waste whenever possible.

24 25 26 27 28 29 30 7 6 5 4 3 2 1

For Jane

Contents

INTRODUCTION

I encountered the WPA Narratives for the first time as a teacher. I had been working with a curriculum that used excerpts from some of these narratives to paint a positive picture of slavery: elderly, rheumy-eyed "uncles" and "aunties" (the interviewers' words, not mine) who desperately missed the "good old days" on the plantation, with masters and mistresses who never abused them, fed them well, and taught them about Jesus.

The quotes left me less than thrilled. And the more I learned about how they had been collected, the more obvious it seemed to me that these narratives could not be trusted.

Slave Narratives: A Folk History of Slavery in the United States from Interviews with Former Slaves is a seventeen-volume work consisting of over three thousand interviews collected from the formerly enslaved during the 1930s. They were gathered as part of the Federal Emergency Relief Agency arm of the New Deal. The WPA (Works Progress Administration) Federal Art Project was established to create employment opportunities for white-collar workers—writers, artists, actors, musicians, and so forth.

These interviews were conducted in Alabama, Arkansas, Florida, Georgia, Mississippi, Maryland, Kentucky, Kansas, Indiana, Oklahoma, Ohio, North and South Carolina, Missouri, Virginia, Texas, and Tennessee. Although they had a broad reach, the interviewers didn't go into every area of slaveholding states, and some regions are notably absent. Some states also have many more interviews represented in the project than others.

The narratives were mostly collected by middle-class white women who were interviewing Black people—most of whom had been children during slavery. Sometimes the interviewers were well-known members of the interviewees' own communities, even relatives of those who had once enslaved them.

A great many of those interviewed were living in the abject poverty of the Great Depression, compounded by the racial violence and fraught power dynamics of the Jim Crow era.

In *The Souls of Womenfolk*, historian Alexis Wells-Oghoghomeh shares:

> The circumstances surrounding the production of the WPA narratives of formerly enslaved African Americans frequently yield questions about how historians use the narratives to reconstruct enslaved southerners' lives. As numerous scholars have discussed, the prevalence of White southerners among the interviewers, the advanced age of the interviewees, and the racist editorializing of the published interviews call into question the historical accuracy of the narratives. For these reasons, some have chosen to use the narratives sparingly.[1]

"For these reasons, some have chosen to use the narratives sparingly." And for this reason, I was incredibly skeptical of using the narratives myself or commending their use to others. Remember, as an educator, I'd seen just how they could be utilized to dull the devastating impact of chattel slavery.

One day, I shared my reservations with my dear friend Abena (whom I like to call my "historian in residence," if "residence" is in my text messages). It resulted in one of our very first disagreements. Abena's work focuses on digging for the stories and perspectives of the enslaved in underutilized source material. And if there was ever an example of underutilized source material, she informed me, it was the WPA Narratives.

We went back and forth, me citing all the ways the narratives had been misused in the past, and Abena understanding my reservations while pointing out that misuse does not render something inherently useless. We then shelved the conversation for several months, but I kept learning and researching. Abena finished her PhD. I applied for grad school. We both continued writing and researching and talking and growing.

And then I came back to her and told her how desperately I wanted to write about enslaved family relationships and that I wished there was a way to find out more about the interior lives of the enslaved.

"This is where the WPA Narratives would prove incredibly useful," she told me.

This time, I listened.

I found the complete series available on Project Gutenberg, downloaded the ebooks onto my Kindle, and began to read. And it was hard. For one thing, many of the interviewers copied down stories with sloppy attempts at capturing dialect that renders some words and phrases almost completely illegible. And for another, in interviews from certain states I just kept running into the same "slavery was better than life is now" rhetoric that had turned me off the narratives in the first place.

But this time, I kept going and started to think more like a historian and less like a casual reader. I saw the spaces where the enslaved hedged a bit with their answers: "*My* master was kind, but I did hear stories about *other* masters who weren't." I saw places where interviewers asked leading questions: "Slavery wasn't all bad, was it?" I saw spots where the desperation of the Great Depression shone through: "I miss slavery because I got to eat every day."

I also saw that the ethnicity of the interviewer sometimes made all the difference. To a white interviewer in Georgia, an enslaved person might say that slavery hadn't been all that bad. To a Black interviewer in Tennessee, they might give a different, less filtered story.

A new picture began to develop for me, even with the limitations of the narratives. And I saw why Abena and Wells-Oghoghomeh still found them useful, despite how they have been misapplied. Especially for a historian who wants to know more about enslaved family life and enslaved womanhood. As Wells-Oghoghomeh shares:

> Women authored only 12 percent of the published narratives produced by formerly enslaved people, yet they constituted an estimated 50 percent of the WPA interviewees. The WPA narratives remain one of the only primary sources through which to access the voices of formerly enslaved girls and women in the anglophone Lower South. As such, studying women's interiority requires historians to reexamine Western epistemological concepts of memory, which prioritize written documents over oral sources and individual recollection over communal reinterpretation in claims about facticity and memory.

She continues:

> Taking seriously many captive Africans' emergence from oral contexts and the continued importance of orality in African American cultures, I read the WPA sources through West African concepts of memory. Scholars Babacar Fall and Alice Bellagamba assert that West Africans' oral histories evince layers of recollection from varied sources and, accordingly, an awareness of the fallibility of individual memory. *People collect knowledges and histories over time, via experience and comparisons to similar accounts, which offer a basis for the integration or rejection of new threads.*[2]

The idea of the WPA Narratives as threads of memory stuck with me as I began to conceptualize this project. I started taking them not just as individual tales plucked from a memory here or there but as a beautiful tapestry forming before my eyes. They are different strokes in a larger painting that begins to stand out in starker relief the more the artist works.

I became obsessed with these stories, poring over thousands of them. What started as work for a project became a passion that filled hours of additional research. I told my husband, "I knew writing about these narratives would change me, but I didn't know I was stumbling upon what I wanted to study for the rest of my life."

The more I read, the more unwieldy the details became. One could write an entire graduate thesis about them (and, at this writing, I am currently doing so). But how could I distill these details for a popular audience? How could I capture three thousand stories in a book for people who probably don't love this stuff enough to get an entire graduate degree but still want to understand what life was really like for the enslaved?

That's when Little Bit was born.

Little Bit is not a real person, at least not in a biographical sense. Her name changes as her story changes, from Little Bit to Lonely One to Lovely One.[3] She's a composite sketch of the many stories I read as I made my way through more than two thousand narratives. For me, she's the picture on the tapestry that is carefully woven together by these narratives.

The book you hold is, at its heart, a compilation of WPA Narratives. But the heroine who starts as Little Bit and ends as Grandmama is your guide. Her story is the common thread that weaves thousands of other stories together. Her narrative is the heartbeat pumping lifeblood through this entire work.

Throughout this book, I will alternate between the composite story of our main character and stories from the WPA Narratives, interspersed with other types of testimony of the formerly enslaved. Sometimes, quotes will be scattered throughout our heroine's story, and at other times, I will draw out the stories that stood out during my research. The main narrative lies somewhere between fiction and nonfiction. Little Bit is nameless because her stories could be anyone's, but the quotes from the WPA Narratives and other firsthand sources are true. The names are real and so very important.

My hope is that this book will bring history to life for you and give new life to the WPA Narratives. They are not without fault, but they are a unique opportunity to examine the interior lives of people whose stories have so often been told by others. If we can look past the biases of compilers and dig into the commonalities between these testimonies and our composite sketch, I think we'll encounter a beautiful picture of love, resilience, and faithfulness.

These narratives provide important insights about enslaved life: worship, education, family, trauma, navigating power dynamics with enslavers, routines, and so much more. They have already been utilized by a wide variety of expert historians, and I add my voice to theirs as both historian and artist, a lover of facts and a lover of story. Little Bit would not be allowed to exist in any of my grad school papers, but the beauty of being a writer is that one can meld the academic and the artistic.

It's an unconventional way to teach history, yes, but I also hope that it's an effective way to *learn* history and see the beauty, humanity, and heart of each and every story I've sampled here.

One last note: this book is dedicated to Jane, whom I will share more about in chapter 6. She was my great-great-great-great-grandmother, the first enslaved woman on my mother's side whom I can name. There were so many women who came before her whose names have been lost to history. In choosing not to name Little Bit, I am honoring them through one story of what might have been. They represent rich interior lives, hopes, dreams, sorrows, joys, loss, sufferings, and triumphs we might never get to know this side of heaven.

Little Bit's name might have been the same as any of my enslaved matriarchs, paternal or maternal: Evaline, Angeline, Sarah, or Jane. But even if the events of Little Bit's life do not mirror the exact order of a single historical life, they *did* happen over the course of several lifetimes that were recorded in those narratives over eighty years ago. And seeing glimpses of what might have been for my mother's mother's mother's mother's mother along the way has been a beautiful, spiritual experience I will never take for granted.

Between my husband and me, we have one living grandparent. That's it. So many of our stories have been lost to history. In passing down Little Bit's tale, I'm also passing down the threads that contribute to the tapestry of the Black, formerly enslaved experience of so many Americans today. I hope that my pen has been faithful. I pray that God has guided my imagination toward the truth of what might have been in my own heritage. And I anxiously await the day I will ask my mothers all about it in glory.

AUTHOR'S NOTE

As stated in the introduction, I've combined some testimonies from the WPA Narratives to create a central narrative for you to follow. However, throughout Little Bit's story, you will find asides guiding you to the sources of certain subjects. These asides are the text's inspiration, and as I have taken a bit of creative liberty in the formatting of this story, I felt they were important to include.

In this work, I have chosen to reference Project Gutenberg's online collection of these narratives (unless otherwise indicated) because I want readers to see how accessible these stories are. Although *I* feel like each one is a beautiful discovery, I have not discovered them. They have been available in public record for longer than I have been alive. I am approaching them to add my voice to an already-existent chorus, and in the course of each chapter will inject my own commentary. When shifting from Little Bit's story to the historical record, I will use the phrase "collective witness." And when you see a name used, that's a true story. My narrative additions will not use traditional names.

I have also taken the liberty of removing a lot of the dialect from the WPA quotes, simply for readability (replacing "wuz" with "was," "de" with "the," "dey" with "they," and so on), but I have not fundamentally changed the stories in any other way. And as always with my work, feel free to check the sources cited in the endnotes. It was important to me that the WPA Narratives remain front and center while moving through Little Bit's story. Think of it as a middle school math worksheet where the teacher asks their students to *show their work*. That's what these narratives included throughout Little Bit's narrative aim to do. I want the reader to see exactly where these details came from and how the story was built as I read and learned and listened.

Last, the epithet *nigger* is replete throughout the WPA Narratives. While I recognize it is important to share the narratives in their fullest sense, I write very conscious of the fact that the primary readers of this book will likely be white, and I will not spell out this word in full. It has gone from being widely used to describe Black people in the South to being something limited to discussion within the Black community. I don't believe there's one right answer to how to use it when quoting primary sources—but for my part, the discussion thereof will stay in the realm of family business.

CHAPTER ONE

Little Bit

It's queer to me, I cannot remember one word my mother said to me, not nary a word she said can I remember.

Joe High, North Carolina

They sold my sister Lucy and my brother Fred in slavery time, and I have never seen 'em in my life. Mother would cry when she was tellin' me 'bout it. She never seen 'em anymore. I just couldn't bear to hear her tell it without crying.

Lizza Baker, North Carolina

She moved through the world like every other child her age—curious, openhearted, innocent, and achingly vulnerable. Soft, dimpled hands, round cheeks, bowlegged gait, and ten little toes sinking deep into the earth, grounding her in the life that was her birthright.

Dawn of Memory

Like every child who came before and every child who would follow, Little Bit started understanding patterns as her eyes adjusted to the wonder of the world around her. Each new experience formed her in ways both large and seemingly infinitesimal. She learned something new every day, her entire existence expanding with each lesson.

It began with a simple collection of touches: lying at her mother's breast throughout the day, nestled up beside her; Auntie setting her in a basket in the side yard where she watched older children toddle naked in the overgrown lawn, chasing the chickens; her first tastes of pot likker and goat's milk to tide her over while Mama was away; Mama's periodic returns to nurse her throughout the day; Auntie's incessant humming, which sometimes broke into words.

> Sometimes I feel like a motherless child,
> Sometimes I feel like a motherless child,
> Sometimes I feel like a motherless child,
> A long way from home, a long way from home.
> Sometimes I feel like I'm almost done,
> Sometimes I feel like I'm almost done,
> Sometimes I feel like I'm almost done,
> And a long, long way from home, a long way from home.

Little Bit first felt the bite of sadness when Auntie sang that mournful song. It burrowed behind her fragile breastbone, filling her tiny chest with a longing she could not name. The same sadness must have welled up in Auntie too, because eventually it would break open and spill out, and tears would shimmer in Auntie's eyes as she gazed into the distance.

Motherless child.

At times, Little Bit recognized that same sadness in Mama's eyes as Mama looked down at her. And those grooves of memory forming in Little Bit's heart and mind were etched deeper still with every look, every touch, every whispered prayer over her small, soft body.

She remembered happy things too, like Papa's visits every Wednesday and Saturday, and the way he'd throw her up in the air. Mama would fuss at him to *put my baby down* with sternness dressed in a warm smile.

> When my Mammy and Daddy got married Marse Henry wouldn't sell Mammy, and Marse Billie wouldn't sell Daddy, so that didn't get to see one another but twice a week—that was on Wednesday and Saturday nights—till after the war was done over. I can still 'member Daddy comin' over to Marse Henry's plantation to see us. (Jasper Battle, Georgia)[1]

Long past those early days, as toddlerhood verged into childhood, Little Bit would remember when Mama let her tag along to the cotton fields. Mama would set her down on a quilt in the thick of them, the stalks swallowing her up, and pretend she didn't know *where oh where has my little baby gone?*

> Very devoted to his mother, he would follow her into the cotton field as she picked or hoed cotton, urged by the thrashing of the overseer's lash. (Squires Jackson, Florida)[2]

She would recall the other children weaving their way through those same fields to bring water to Mama and the others while they worked or running to and from the Big House with messages from Missus to the overseer.

"ALL I CAN REMEMBER"

I 'members the days when mammy wore a blue handkerchief 'round her head an' cooked in the great house. She'd sometimes sneak me a cookie or a cobbler and fruits. She had her own little garden an' a few chickens and we would of been happy 'cept that we was scared of bein' sold. (Charlie Barbour, North Carolina)[3]

The first thing [Henry Bland] remembers of his parents is when he was quite small and was allowed to remain in the master's kitchen in the "big house" where his mother was cook. (Henry Bland, Georgia)[4]

All that I can 'member is, that I was just a little tot running 'round, and I would always watch for my mother to come home. I was always glad to see her, for the day was long and I knew she'd cook something for me to eat. I can remember that as good as 'twas yesterday. (Jessie Rowell, Florida)[5]

Little Bit would remember Mama returning from the fields on the days when she was made to stay behind. Like Auntie, Mama sang many different tunes, but Little Bit's favorite was:

No more auction block for me
No more, no more
No more auction block for me
Many thousands gone

She would remember Mama staying up late, working on one of the quilts that were ubiquitous in Little Bit's life: as a partition in their one-room cabin, as the blanket on their narrow bed, as the little scrap of fabric Little Bit carried around in her hands since she was a baby, careworn and well-loved. So many nights, she fell asleep while her mother quilted by candlelight, watching the shadows dance on the cabin's walls.

Log cabins had dirt floor, sometimes plankin' down. I worked late and made pretty quilts. (Elvira Boles, Texas)[6]

She would also remember Mama rising early each day to greet the morning with a prayer of thanksgiving. Those early supplications by the light of a candle formed Little Bit in ways her mother could never have imagined. Her mother's prayers were Little Bit's first step in a long journey of discovering the Almighty. Of making peace with him.

"THE SLAVES WEREN'T ALLOWED TO GO TO CHURCH"

Duncan always listened for his mother's return from the field, which was heralded by a song, no matter how tired she was. (Duncan Gaines, Florida)[7]

It seemed to the child that he had just gone to bed when the old tallow candle was lighted and his "pappy" arose and fell upon his knees and prayed aloud for God's blessings and thanked him for another day. The field hands were to be in the field by five o'clock and it meant to rise before day, summer and winter. Not so bad in summer for it was soon day but in winter the weather was cold and darkness was longer passing away. When daylight came field hands had been working an hour or more. (Randall Lee, Florida)[8]

I member hearing my mammy pray "Oh Father open up the doors and show us." I'd look up to the ceiling to see if he was gonna open up something; silly, silly me, thinking such. (Sylvia Lee, Tennessee)[9]

The slaves weren't 'lowed to go to church, but they would whisper 'round and all meet in the woods and pray. The only time I 'members my pa was one time when I was a little chile, he set me on a log by him an' prayed, an' I knows that was where the seeds of religion was planted in my mind. (Adeline Hodges, Alabama)[10]

Little Bit's memories would be as warm as Mama could make them. As warm as the well-loved quilt they would lie under together every night, Little Bit bending herself to fit into the grooves of Mama's soft, welcoming frame. Later, when she added these memories up, they were far too few—scant offerings of a mother whose child was never fully her own. There was never enough time in the gathering darkness of night and the growing light of day—not enough for them to be together the way they wished.

Not enough for them to be together the way they *ought* to have been.

Where oh where has my baby gone?

Little Bit's memories would be shaped as much by her mother's scars as her mother's words. Every morning, she watched as Mama dressed, throwing on her plain cotton shift, easing it over her strong, protective frame. The same tallow candle that lit Mama's morning prayers illuminated the constellations on her back: long, raised welts from a bullwhip just like the one that hung from the overseer's belt. Sometimes, Little Bit would open her eyes to see Daddy down for a visit, rubbing a salve on Mama's back to ease the pain, the smell of the beef tallow causing her stomach to rumble. Sometimes, she would watch him bend, his forehead hitting the base of Mama's neck where it met her back, and in the dim light of the candle, his tears would fall on her scars.

"THE CRY OF MY POOR MOTHER"

Oliver Bell says the first thing he remembers was seeing his mother whipped. (Oliver Bell, Alabama)[11]

I saw Old Bates whip my mother once for leaving her finger print in the pone bread when she patted it down before she put it into the oven. (Frank Bates, Florida)[12]

I sure has seen my mammy and lots more get whuppins. (Tom Bates, Mississippi)[13]

I seen my mama whooped. (Mattie Fannen, Arkansas)[14]

My mother was a field hand, and one morning was ten or fifteen minutes behind the others in getting into the field. As soon as she reached the spot where they were at work, the overseer commenced whipping her. She cried, "Oh! Pray—Oh! Pray—Oh! Pray"—these are generally the words of slaves, when imploring mercy at the hands of their oppressors. I heard her voice and knew it, and jumped out of my bunk and went to the door. Though the field was some distance from the house, I could hear every crack of the whip and every groan and cry of my poor mother. I remained at the door, not daring to venture any farther. The cold chills ran over me, and I wept aloud. After giving her ten lashes, the sound of the whip ceased, and I returned to my bed and found no consolation but in my tears. It was not yet daylight. (William Wells Brown, Missouri)[15]

Sometimes her memories would be shaped by her mother's loss—her mother's tears. Little Bit would learn the contours of heartbreak from watching her mother experience it again and again and again. She would learn to feel every missing space where a loved one used to be.

Mama was a *motherless child* like Auntie, and though she didn't sing the song in Little Bit's presence, the small girl felt the song when she noticed Mama's longing. Mama always smiled when she caught Little Bit looking, opening her arms so that her daughter could run into them. Little Bit hugged Mama as tightly as she could, mending a constantly breaking heart the only way she knew how.

"THAT BROUGHT GRIEF TO MY PARENTS"

My oldest brother was sold to Virginia and shipped down into Texas about ten years before I was born and I ain't never seen him. (Norman Burkes, Arkansas)[16]

My parents and four children was sold and left six children behind. They kept the oldest children. In that way I was sold but never alone. Our family was divided and that brought grief to my parents. (John W. H. Barnett, Arkansas)[17]

My mother's mother was taken from her and sold when she was a baby. (Salena Taswell, Florida)[18]

Mama said she was sold once, away from her mother, but they let her have her four children. She grieved for her old mama, 'fraid she would have a hard time. (Katherine Clay, Arkansas)[19]

All these things—these words, these sights, these sounds, these smells—would work together to form Little Bit into the person she would become. Before she could speak ten words, she was soaking in life around her like a sponge, learning the boundaries and the bounty that lay in the life to which she'd been born.

Her mother's touch to start and end each day—and the lack of that touch in the intervening hours. Her father's presence once or twice a week—and his absence while he worked on another plantation. Her siblings' voices all around her—and their absence when they were there one day and sold the next. Her mother's smiles and laughter and play—her mother's tears and groans and work.

Little Bit's world grew every single day, adding details to the picture framed by the realities of human bondage. She saw it clearly as it took shape—her place in the world, her mother's inability to protect that space, and all the while, Auntie's singing:

Mammy, is Ol' Massa gonna sell us tomorrow?
Yes, my chile.
Where he gonna sell us?
'Way down South in Georgia.

COLLECTIVE WITNESS: REMEMBERING FEAR

Henry could not remember his mother's face. Every detail he held, his older sister had relayed to him, her heart seeming to break with each telling of the story.

He knew he shouldn't ask her, as reliving the memory ripped open a wound caused by his own curiosity, but ask again he did. Ever since he could form the words, he'd asked. And Sister had answered, as if she knew the only thing she could offer the motherless child was the solace of knowing that his mother hadn't meant to leave him.

Sister wasn't supposed to see their mother sold. She'd been crouching behind the Big House, toddler in her arms, straining to catch the last of Mama. Sister watched them pull Mama toward the gate, caught her one last, tearful look back at child and toddler, knowing she would never see them again in this life.

Henry didn't know it though. It was a long time before he stopped toddling out to the gate on his soft, bare feet, looking toward the place where they'd hauled his mammy away, waiting to see if she would come home.

Henry didn't remember watching his mother leave, but he did remember being punished for trying to find her.[20]

Duncan waited for his mother too. Every day, he waited at the edge of the cotton fields for her, listening for the inevitable song she'd sing when she arrived. No matter how tired she was, her voice rose in one of the familiar melodies of Duncan's childhood:

> She was very fond of her children and did not share the attitude of many slave mothers who thought of their children as belonging solely to the masters. She lived in constant fear that "old marse Seever" would meet with some adversity and be forced to sell them separately. She always whispered to them about "the war" and fanned to a flame their desire to be free. (Duncan Gaines, Florida)[21]

Duncan and his family were sold many times, and despite his mother's constant fear, they always wound up sold together—parents George and Martha Gaines along with their four children. When freedom came in 1865, Duncan was twelve years old and still nestled safely in his family unit.

Duncan and Henry had very different childhoods, but they were both traumatic. Duncan and his family remained together but lived under constant threat of being ripped apart, a credible threat one or both of Duncan's parents had most likely experienced during their enslavement. A conservative estimate states that roughly *half* of all enslaved people were separated from their spouses and parents; about one in four of those sold were children.[22]

Charlie Barbour was fourteen years old when the Civil War ended. He had barely been old enough to partake in the backbreaking labor he watched his parents do every day in the fields. He remembered shooting marbles and playing hide-and-seek with other children. When "the grown folks" had time, they sometimes had "dances an' sometimes corn shuckin's."

If one were to read only part of Charlie's story, they might even be able to imagine a benign form of bondage that many a WPA interviewer wanted so desperately to paint. One where, yes, people were divided harshly along lines of race and gender, freedom and bondage, but the enslaved were treated "just like family." They were "well taken care of" and lived carefree lives outside of the responsibilities of their labor.

But at eighty-six, Charlie still remembered the same dread that haunted Duncan's mother, Martha Gaines:

> Yes'm, I reckon I was glad to get free, 'cause I knows then that I won't wake up some morning to find that my mammy or some of the rest of my family am done sold. I left the day I heard 'bout the surrender and I fared right good, though I knows them what ain't faring so well. (Charlie Barbour, North Carolina)[23]

Charlie's worst fear *did* happen to Viney Baker, who was only six years old when the Civil War ended. Her first memories were still solidifying, plotting to form her into the woman she would become:

> One night I lay down on the straw mattress with my mammy, an' the next morning I woked up and she was gone. When I asked

> 'bout her I finds that a speculator come there the night before and wanted to buy a woman. They had come and got my mammy without waking me up. I always been glad somehow that I was asleep. (Viney Baker, North Carolina)[24]

Folklorist Ruby Pickens Tartt interviewed a woman named Laura Clark who had been very much awake when separated from her mother. Tartt described Clark as "black and wrinkled," and moving "limpingly" around her porch:

> Battered cans and rickety boxes were filled with a profusion of flowers of the common variety. Laura offered me a split-bottomed chair and lowered herself slowly into a rocker that creaked even under her frail body. "Poorly, Miss, poorly," she responded to my query about her health. "Ain't like the old days. I's crippled and most blind now, after all the years what I got."

But for all her agedness, Clark still remembered being separated from her mother when she was six:

> I recollect Mammy said to old Julie, "Take care my baby child (that was me), and iffen I never sees her no more raise her for God." Then she fell off the wagon where us was all settin' and roll over on the ground just a'cryin'. But us was eatin' candy what they done give us for to keep us quiet, and I didn't have sense enough to know what ailed Mammy, but I knows now and I never seed her no more in this life. (Laura Clark, Alabama)[25]

Duncan, Henry, Charlie, Viney, Laura—these and so many others existed on a broad spectrum of loss. Whether they were robbed of their parents' literal presence via sale or robbed of the innocence of a secure attachment with them, they all felt the ways that slavery stole from them the privilege of peaceful early memories.

The First Loss

Little Bit spent most of her time separated from her mother out of sheer necessity. During her formative years of attachment and bonding, she was most often ferried to other caretakers to let Mama work from "can't see to can't see," her labor enriching not her child's future inheritance or their life together but the enslaver whose greed could one day tear them apart.

The child's days were spent with other children, being watched either by a granny who was too old to work or a mother who had proved her worth to the master by bearing so many children she was allowed to help raise the others.

When Little Bit was in the stage of deepest attachment to her mama—crying when the older woman had to leave her with someone else for the day—there was no time for coddling or prolonged goodbyes. Mama had a job to do. And while part of her job was increasing the master's estate by bearing him children who padded his wealth in labor or cash flow, *raising* those children was not part of her job description. In fact, eventual separation from that child might be inevitable.

"I SEEN SEPARATION OF CHILD AND MOTHER"

I have seen the separation of husband and wife, child and mother, and the extreme grief of those involved and the lash administered to a grieving slave for neglecting their work. (Henry H. Buttler, Texas)[26]

He'd sell a man here and the woman there and if they's children, he'd sell 'em someplace else. (Andy Anderson, Texas)[27]

I seed women and little children crying and begging not to be separated, but it didn't do no good. They had to go. (Sterlin Arwine, Texas)[28]

I seed chillun too little to walk from they mammies sold right off the block in Woodville. They was sold just like calfs. (Josie Brown, Texas)[29]

Little Bit had never seen an auction when the speculator came to her enslaver's farm. She was just three years old, toddling in the side yard with the other children, naked as a jaybird in the hot August sun, when she saw a strange white man at a distance. He was eyeing the folks working between the rows of corn, backs bent against the sticky Mississippi heat.

She felt the tension in the air, heard Auntie's sharp intake of breath, watched tired shoulders stiffen as the white man passed them by. Her little mind whirred, trying to understand the possibility before her. The other children whispered that he was a speculator. Little Bit had heard stories of speculators before, and they seemed as scary as her master's huge, drooling hunting dogs in her mind's eye, but this man didn't have any fangs. He was just a regular white man.

> Oh, that was a terrible time! All the slaves be in the field, blowing, hoeing, singing in the boiling sun. Ole Marse, he come through the field with the man called the speculator. They walked round just looking, just looking. All the darks know what this mean. They didn't dare look up, just work right on. Then the speculator, he see who he want. He talk to Old Marse, then they slaps the handcuffs on him and take him away to the cotton country. Oh, them was awful times. When the speculator was ready to go with the slaves, if there was any who didn't want to go, he'd thrash 'em, then tie 'em behind the wagon and make 'em run till they fell on the ground, then he'd thrash 'em till they say they'll go without no trouble. (Sarah Gudger, North Carolina)[30]

When the speculator came to the side yard to look at the children, Little Bit met his curious gaze with a bold and inquisitive one of her own, wondering who he was to interrupt the status quo of her early childhood days. It wasn't until she heard her mother's piercing scream that she started to panic.

The man pointed at her, and her enslaver said, "Three hundred dollars."

That number seemed to suit the speculator just fine.

Mama was running from the field, screaming, sobbing, keening, begging. Little Bit's lip began to tremble. Mama threw herself on the ground at their enslaver's feet; to him it was a mere tantrum.

Their enslaver looked down at Mama, lips curled in the same look of disgust that Little Bit had seen Missus give to curdled milk or a full slop jar. He motioned to the overseer, who had followed closely on Mama's heels with an unsheathed whip.

Little Bit understood now, and she started to cry too. Auntie shushed her, soothed her, but Little Bit was terrified now because the speculator *was* the monster she'd heard about. She wailed for her mother, little arms reaching toward their first source of comfort in this life, clawing toward the heart of her very first memories, the axis of her ever-expanding world.

Mama reached out too, heedless of the overseer who was bringing down his whip on her already crisscrossed back. Mama reached out for her last child, the sweet, vulnerable little girl she'd carried, nestled beneath her heartbeat, breathing as one.

But their love wasn't strong enough to hold them together.

COLLECTIVE WITNESS: THE HIGHEST BIDDER

Millie Williams was "just a little thing" the first time she was sold, which was to Hal Birdon along with her mother, Martha, and her sister Catherine. Shortly after Martha was sold to "Master Birdon," she gave birth to another child, a little girl whom Millie would report she didn't remember much about because Millie was sold again so soon after.

While she lived with her mother, Millie remembered caring for the little girl:

> I'd 'member that many a time I'd take her to the field where my mama was workin', I'd take her there to nurse. Then I'd 'member the time my mama come in from the field for water, she come 'round the back way an' I'd go meet her with the baby. The mistress, she caught my mama an' told her if she ever come in 'gain she would tell the master. When I'd sold back to Master Benford, I'd never seen my folks no more.[31]

Millie's experience being sold was traumatic, even in her eighty-six-year-old memory:

> After I was sold back to Master Benford, he puts me in the n—— yard. That's where the master kept slaves he traded. It was just a bunch of shacks thrown together and dirty was no name for it, it was worse than a pig pen. The man that watch over us in the n—— yard was the meanest man that ever lived. He would take a club and beat the daylights out of us. The club didn't leave no scars like the bullwhip and didn't bring the price down when we is sold.
>
> One day Master Benford takes us to town and puts us on that auction block and a man by the name of Bill Dunn bought me. I was 'bout seven years old. Talkin' 'bout somethin' awful, you should have been there. The slave owners was shoutin' an' sellin' the children to one man an' they mama and pappy to another. The slaves cries and takes on something awful. If a woman had lots of children she was sold for more, 'cause it a sign she a good breeder. (Millie Williams, Texas)[32]

At seven, Millie would have been far from the youngest enslaved person auctioned off in this manner. Josie Brown of Texas remembered, "I seen children too little to walk from they mammies sold right off the block." Harriet Hill was just three years old the first time she was sold away from her mother.

> I been sold in my life twice to my knowing. I was sold away from my dear old mammy at three years old but I can remember it. I remembers it. It like selling a calf from the cow. Exactly, but we are human beings and ought to be better than to do such. I was too little to remember my price. I was sold to be a nurse maid. They bought me and took me on away that time. The next time they put me up in a wagon and auctioned me off. That time I didn't sell. (Harriet Hill, Arkansas)[33]

"We are human beings and ought to be better than to do such," Harriet told interviewer Irene Robertson.

As a woman in her eighties, Harriet was able to reflect on the harsh practice of separating small children from their parents and turning their most formative memories into nightmares. But at age three, Harriet was just starting to be formed into the person she would become, tracing the contours of the world she inhabited. And the lesson she would have picked up standing on the auction block was that she was only worth whatever price the highest bidder was willing to pay.

Memory and Identity

Famous abolitionist Frederick Douglass was at a similarly young age when his mother paid him one of her very last visits. She took the twelve-mile trek on foot to see him whenever she was able, and Frederick looked back fondly on their reunions.

"One of the visits of my mother to me, while at Col. Lloyd's," Douglass recalls, "I remember very vividly, as affording a bright gleam of a mother's love, and the earnestness of a mother's care."

On this day, Douglass had somehow upset the cook, Aunt Katy. In her ire, she withheld his meals for an entire day, leaving the starving young boy to sob behind the house in his hunger. Finally, at sundown, Douglass could bear it no longer. He went inside and snuck an ear of corn into the fire to roast enough to eat. He was just taking the corn out when his mother walked in:

> There was pity in her glance at me, and a fiery indignation at Aunt Katy at the same time; and, while she took the corn from me, and gave me a large ginger cake, in its stead, she read Aunt Katy a lecture which she never forgot.

Douglass, used to fending for himself, was at last being protected by an adult who loved him. He remembered further:

> That night I learned the fact, that I was not only a child, but somebody's child. The "sweet cake" my mother gave me was in the shape of a heart, with a rich, dark ring glazed upon the edge of it. I was victorious, and well off for the moment; prouder, on my mother's knee, than a king upon his throne.[34]

"I was not only a child, but *somebody's* child."

The formative, identity-shaping moments of a mother's love should be administered as often as possible, but Douglass and countless other children were robbed of them for the greater parts of their childhoods because of the greed of their enslavers. Instead, these moments were shaped by violence, scarcity, and loss. For one night, Douglass got to feel the way every child should feel: safe and secure in the arms of a mother who would move heaven and earth to protect him.

That was the last visit he remembered before his mother died.

Memory's Lessons

Most psychologists believe the average person's first memory occurs between the ages of two and four. These are years when children start to form their view of the world, asking questions like, Is it beautiful? Is it fun? Is it loving? Is it safe?

The vast majority of those interviewed for the WPA Narratives of the 1930s were mere children when they experienced the realities of slavery. A great many of them called to mind memories from that "first memory" window of ages two to eight. Some of their stories end in beautiful reunions:

> After freedom my mammy come from Lebanon and got me. I'll never forget that day. (Frankie Goole, Tennessee)[35]

Some end like Millie Willams's story:

> I'd never seen my folks no more.

Anna Baker was blessed to see her mother again. She was very young when her mother ran away to avoid unwanted advances from the overseer, and only seven years old when her mother returned to collect her after the war. Anna did not have a first memory of her mother to share, at least not one she was fully conscious of. But she did remember this meeting:

> She came out of the house to get us and at first I was scared of her 'cause I didn't know who she was. But she put me up in her lap and loved me and I knowed then that I loved her. (Anna Baker, Mississippi)[36]

Anna knew her mother not by sight but by the feeling of love and safety that the older woman provided when she held her. She remembered that feeling from the time she was just a Little Bit of a thing, held tightly to her mother's chest, trusting the older woman to help her navigate the wide, new world. And by God's grace, her mama was able to come back into her life and do just that.

CHAPTER TWO

Lonely One

> See this face? See this mouth all twisted over here so's I can't shut it? See that eye? All red, ain't it? Been that way for eighty-some years now. Guess it's gonna stay that way till I die. . . . That's what slave days was like.
>
> Henrietta King, Virginia

> They jus' have a old frame with planks to sleep on and no mattress or nothin'. In winter they have to keep the fire goin' all night to keep from freezin'. They put a old quilt down on the floor for the li'l folks. They have a li'l trough us used to eat out of with a li'l wooden paddle. Us didn't know nothin' 'bout knives and forks.
>
> Ellen Butler, Texas

If she was careful, she could go the whole day without inciting the wrath of Missus.

To an outsider, that might not seem like such an incredible feat. Her Missus was the finest lady in town, renowned in the community for her gentility and hospitality. When they had guests, she cooed over many a young "pickaninny,"[1] going on and on about how it was her heart's duty to make a home for any motherless colored child, calling them her "pets" and rubbing the tops of their heads with her signature mixture of thinly veiled disgust and magnanimous condescension.

Yet even with all of the public attention from Missus, Little Bit grew into Lonely One, forever aching for her mother's touch.

The Children's House

Lonely One didn't like having her head rubbed, but she preferred it to having a brush launched at her, a pot full of hot water tossed in her direction, or her underarm—the only still-supple part of her ravenously hungry frame—mercilessly pinched. When she *didn't* have company, Missus stalked around the house adorned in her wealthy-planter's-wife finery, but she had a foul mouth and would just as soon cuss Lonely One out as bid her good morning.

"OLD MASTER TREATED US SLAVES BAD"

I'd say old master treated us slaves bad and there was one thing I couldn't understand, 'cause he was religious and every Sunday morning everybody had to get ready and go for prayer. . . . Sometimes he get up off his knees and before we get out the house he cuss us out. (Carey Davenport, Texas)[2]

No'm, they weren't no good times at his house. He was a widower an' his daughter kept house for him. I nursed for her, and one day I was playing with the baby. It hurt its li'l hand and commenced to cry, an' she whirl on me, pick up a hot iron an' run it all down my arm and hand. It took off the flesh when she done it. (Delia Garlic, Alabama)[3]

When I was about nine years old, for about six months, I slept on a crocus bag sheet in order to get up and nurse the babies when they cried. Do you see this finger? You wonder why it's broke? Well one night the babies cried and I didn't wake up right away to tend to 'em and my mistress jumped out of bed, grabbed the piece of iron that was used to push up the fire and began beating me with it. That's the night this finger got broke, she hit me on it. I have two more fingers she broke beating me at different times. She made me break this leg too. You see they would put the women in stocks and beat 'em whenever they done something wrong. That's the way my leg was broke. (Unnamed Informant, Georgia)[4]

You see, my mamma belong to old William Cleveland and old Polly Cleveland, and they was the meanest two white folks what ever lived, 'cause they was always beating on their slaves. I know, 'cause mamma told me, and I hears about it other places, and besides, old Polly, she was a Polly devil if there ever was one, and she whipped my little sister what was only nine months old and just a baby to death. She come and took the diaper offen my little sister and whipped till the blood just ran—just cause she cry like all babies do, and it kilt my sister. I never forgot that, but I sot some even with that old Polly devil and it's this-a-way. (Mary Armstrong, Texas)[5]

Young Missy wasn't half as bad. Yes, the younger girl was spoiled and petulant, forever bossing Lonely One around and scolding her for not playing a game right, tying a bow incorrectly, or failing to support Missy's tone-deaf vocal performances enthusiastically enough. But she didn't hit Lonely One, and she didn't call her names. Most of the time, she tried to be nice, in her own way.

"She's not your friend," warned Cook, and Lonely One tried to take heed. The older woman had taken the little girl under her wing five years prior when she'd first arrived at the forced labor camp that the white folks called a plantation. "Play her games and heed her wishes, but remember she's not your friend."

But Lonely One was lonely.

Certainly, the older women here had been nothing but welcoming to the young girl when she'd first toddled through the gate, hiccuping and sobbing, missing her mother after a days-long journey to her new state. They'd taken turns passing her around, from house to house, holding her when she cried at night, teaching her the ropes of this new environment, and becoming her fictive kin. She'd even grown to love Cook, the woman who reminded her of her mother, having settled into a routine of frequenting her cabin more than all of the others.

> I was born one night and the very next morning my poor little mammy died. Her name was Lucinda. My pa was William Davenport. When I was a little mite they turned me over to the granny nurse on the plantation. She was the one who tended the pickaninnies. She got a woman to nurse me what had a young baby, so I didn't know no difference. Any woman what had a baby 'bout my age would nurse me, so I groomed up in the quarters well and happy as any child. (Charles Davenport, Mississippi)[6]

For her first three years at the new estate, she lived in the children's house, the cabin reserved for the care of children too young to work in the fields. She helped the grannies rock the cradles, served up the meals in the trough, and carried babies to and from the children's house, entertaining them until their mothers were able to return from the fields and nurse them.

"THE WOMEN HAD IT HARD TOO"

When babies was born old n—— grannies handled them cases, but until they was about three years old they wasn't 'lowed round the quarters, but was wet nursed by women who didn't work in the field and kept in separate quarters and in the evening their mammies were let to see 'em. (Jeptha Choice, Texas)[7]

The women had it hard too; women with little babies would have to go to work in the mornings with the rest, come back, nurse their children and go back to the field, stay two or three hours then go back and eat dinner; after dinner they would have to go to the field and stay two or three more hours then go and nurse the children again, go back to the field and stay till night. One or maybe two old women would stay in a big house and keep all the children while their mothers worked in the fields. (Clayborn Gantling, Florida)[8]

Pappy was a driver under the overseer, but mammy say that she stay at the little nursery cabin and look after all the little babies. That had a cabin fixed up with homemade cradles and things where they put all the babies. Their mammies would come in from the field about ten o'clock to nurse 'em and then later in the day, my mammy would feed the youngest on pot likker and the older ones on greens and pot likker. That had skimmed milk and mush, too, and all of 'em stayed as fat as a butter balls, me among 'em. Mammy saw that I always got my share. (Callie Williams, Alabama)[9]

Lonely One was still Little Bit then, loved on by a community of older women who felt for the motherless child she had become.

But one day, when she was all of six years old, Missus saw how well Little Bit soothed a crying infant who refused to latch for anyone but his mother. She watched as Little Bit bounced with the baby, cooing at him and singing the song Auntie used to sing:

Sometimes I feel like a motherless child,
Sometimes I feel like a motherless child,
Sometimes I feel like a motherless child,
A long way from home, a long way from home.

She sounded far older than her years and far sadder than any six-year-old had the right to be. The grief behind her breastbone had grown heavier than it seemed her fragile frame could carry—and yet she carried it.

The baby looked up at her with curious eyes, stilling his sobs as she swayed. Little Bit knew how it felt to want her mama, even when the arms of others promised all the warmth and safety they could offer a motherless child. He felt that kinship and allowed her to feed him just a little bit of goat's milk to tide him over until his mother was allowed in from the fields to feed her son.

Missus was supposed to be in confinement, her burgeoning belly having long since burst from the shelter of her forever tightening corset. But Marse was out of town, and she insisted on checking in on the field hands herself, even though it was thought unseemly for a white woman to be out and about while expecting.

Enslaved women worked in the fields even when their own bellies were swollen with pregnancy. There was no confinement for them. They were expected to work until their babies were born on top of the cotton, if need be. It had happened more than once that one of the grannies had to leave the children's house and run, knees to chest, to make it to the fields to cut the cord.

> Expectant mothers toiled in the fields until they felt their labor pains. It was not uncommon for babies to be born in the fields. (Sam and Louisa Everett, Florida)[10]

Missus was supposed to have her feet up. Resting. Waiting. Crocheting wee socks or working on a cross-stitch for the nursery. Had she occupied herself with any of these tasks instead of walking outside that day, she may never have seen the little girl calming the howling child.

Missus had been angry when Marse brought that little slip of a girl back from a Mississippi auction block. He'd been haggling over a lot of slaves, and the speculator threw in the toddler as a good faith bonus.

"Her mother has had eleven children in the last fifteen years," her husband told her. "The girl will make a fine breeder someday."

But *someday* wasn't today. So, for now, the little girl would do nicely as a nursemaid for the baby to come.

A New Job

Little Bit was only six years old when Missus decided she would help raise Little Missy. So, alongside the wet nurse Missus selected from among the slaves, Little Bit took her meager belongings—a threadbare blanket and a change of clothes—to the Big House to live.

> White women wouldn't nurse their own babies 'cause it would make their breast fall. They would bring a healthy woman and a clean woman up to the house. They had a house close by. She would nurse her baby and the white baby, too. They would feed her everything she wanted. She didn't have to work 'cause the milk would be hot to give the babies. Dannie and my brother Bradford, and Mary my sister and Miss Maggie nursed my mama. Rich women didn't nurse their babies, never did, 'cause it would cause their breast to be flat. (Betty Curlett, Arkansas)[11]

Nurse suckled the baby, and Little Bit cared for her in every other way—changing her diapers, rocking her when she was fussy, and even carting her from Nurse to Missus and back in the middle of the night. As she grew in age, so did her responsibilities. She fed Missy, bathed Missy, emptied Missy's slop jar, and sat and fanned Missy while Missus read to her.

It was grueling, exhausting work, as Missy's feet were to never hit the ground. Little Bit was expected to take care of her every need. And while Nurse and Cook tried to care for Little Bit, she was often left to her own devices, isolated from everyone else to see to Missy's care. She lay on the floor next to Missy's bed every evening, grateful for the thick quilt Cook had brought from the quarters to serve as her bed. So many nights, she stayed up and stared at the ceiling, fingers playing with the frayed edges of the piece of quilt that was all she had to hold on to of her own mother.

"THE GIRLS NURSED AND WASHED AND IRONED"

Massa have six children when war come on and I nursed all of 'em. I stays in the house with 'em and slept on a pallet on the floor, and soon I's big enough to tote the milk pail they puts me to milking too. Massa have more'n a hundred cows and most the time me and Violet do all the milking. (Katie Darling, Texas)[12]

As I had no brothers or sisters or any other relatives to care for me, my master, who was Mr. Robert Ridley, had me placed in his house where I was taught to wait tables and to do all kinds of housework. Mr. Ridley had a very large plantation, and he raised cotton, corn, oats, wheat, peas, and livestock. Horses and mules were his specialty—I remember that he had one little boy whose job was to break these animals so that they could be easily sold. My job was to wait tables, help with the housecleaning, and act as nursemaid to three young children belonging to the master. (George Womble, Georgia)[13]

The girls swept the yards, cleaned the house, nursed and washed and ironed, combed old miss's and the children's hair, cut their fingers and toenails, and mended their clothes. (Mose Banks, Arkansas)[14]

Little Bit became Lonely One in the Big House. Both Nurse and Cook had families of their own and were allowed to sleep with them in the cabins, but Lonely One remained all times at Missy's feet in case she needed something in the night, which left her always in the pathway of Missus's boundless rage.

Missus was also notoriously stingy with food. Nurse and Cook did not eat while they were at the Big House for fear of being caught in the act. They ate big breakfasts before they came in the morning and downed their dinner when they returned home at night, supplementing their meager rations with morsels from the bountiful gardens they were allowed to care for in their spare time. They often brought food for Lonely One to scarf down before Missus could catch her focusing her attention on something other than serving Missy.

Lonely One learned to eat fast, use the privy fast, even fall asleep fast for fear she would miss one of Missus's or Missy's needs and reap the inevitable *thunk* on the back of her head. She lived in constant terror of the older white woman's disapproval and the violence that usually accompanied it.

The others got Sundays off, but Lonely One was on call at all times, even accompanying the family to worship so she could sit next to Missy and shoo the flies away. Sundays were her hungriest days because she saw neither Cook nor Nurse. She had to make do with the slim rations Missus afforded her—when the woman remembered to feed her at all.

COLLECTIVE WITNESS: **HUNGER**

Hunger did not plague everyone who suffered through enslavement. In fact, many respondents for the WPA Narratives reported having plenty to eat. Still, there were many tales of hunger:

> I lived with good people, my white folks treated us good. There was plenty of 'em that didn't fare as we did. Some of the poor folks almost starved to death. Why the way their masters treated them was scandalous, treated them like cats and dogs. We always had plenty of food, never knowed what it was to want food bad enough to have to steal it like a whole lot of 'em. Master would always give us plenty when he give us our rations. Of course we slaves were given food and clothing and just enough to keep us goin' good. (Sarah Gudger, North Carolina)[15]

> The rich white folks never did no work; they had darkies to do it for them. In the summer we had t' work outdoors, in the winter in the house. I had to card and spin till ten o'clock. Never got much rest, had to get up at four the next morning and start again. Didn't get much

> to eat, nothing, just a little cornbread and molasses. Lady, honey, you can't know what a time I had. All cold and hungry. No'm, I ain't telling no lies. It's the gospel truth. It sho' is. (Mariah Hines, Virginia)[16]

> They didn't half feed us either. They fed the animals better. They gives the mules ruffage and such to chaw on all night. But they didn't give us nothing to chaw on. Learned us to steal, that's what they done. Why we would take anything we could lay our hands on, when we was hungry. Then they'd whip us for lying when we say we don't know nothing about it. But it was easier to stand, when the stomach was full. (Robert Falls, Tennessee)[17]

Henrietta King was just eight or nine years old when her own hunger led to lifelong disfigurement.

Henrietta was age ninety-five when a WPA interviewer sat down to talk with her. Unlike many of those interviewed, she spoke freely, tumbling in and out of stories until she came to the subject of her face.

"See this face?" she said. "See this mouth all twisted over here so's I can't shut it? See that eye? All red, ain't it? Been that way for eighty-some years now. Guess it's gonna stay that way till I die."

To Henrietta, her crumpled face told the interviewer exactly "what slave days was like."

"Missus was so stingy-mean that she didn't put enough on the table to feed a swallow," she said.

One morning, Henrietta's missus put a peppermint on her wash-stand. It was Henrietta's job to empty her missus's slop jar (chamber pot) every morning after eating "little pieces of scrapbook" from the kitchen meant to last her all day. She was so hungry that she snatched up the peppermint and ate it.

When her missus found out what Henrietta had done, she set out to whip the little girl. Henrietta kept running away until Missus called to her daughter to help subdue the child. Eventually, they resorted to shoving Henrietta's head under the leg of a rocking chair, where Missus sat while her daughter carried out the whipping for "near a hour with that rocker leg a-pressin' down on my head."

Henrietta must have lost consciousness, because the next thing she knew, the doctor was there, "a-pushin' and diggin' at my face, but he couldn't do nothin' at all with it. Seem like that rocker pressin' on my young bones had crushed 'em all into soft pulp."

As Henrietta described:

> The next day, I couldn't open my mouth and I feel it and they weren't no bone in the left side at all. And my mouth kept a-slipping over to the right side and I couldn't chew nothing—only drink milk. Well, ole Missus musta got kinda sorry cause she gets the doctor to come regular and pry at my mouth. He gets it after a while so it's open and I could move my lips, but it kept moving over to the right, and he couldn't stop that. After a while it was over just where it is now. And I ain't never groomed no more teeth on that side. Ain't ever been able to chew nothing good since. Don't even remember what it was to chew. Been eating liquid, stews, and soup ever since that day, and that day was eighty-six years ago. (Henrietta King, Virginia)[18]

Henrietta then leaned forward and told her interviewers to touch her face. "That's what slave days was like," she finished.

Virginia director Eudora Ramsay Richardson did not believe this story when it was brought to her by Roscoe Lewis, the director of the Black unit of WPA interviewers in Virginia. She went to Henrietta's house to see for herself what she was sure would be a "gross exaggeration."[19]

Instead, she found that Henrietta's face did, indeed, look just as gruesome as had been described, and Henrietta related the exact same story of how it happened.

A Stolen Education

Lonely One was not horribly disfigured by Missus, but she was constantly berated in ways that made her feel small and useless.

She watched Missy enjoy a beautiful childhood full of dolls and make-believe, plenty of food, and doting affection from her mother. She stood by while Missus catered to her young daughter, offering her everything in the world.

Lonely One was almost eleven when Missus started to teach five-year-old Missy how to read. It was Lonely One's job to sit and fan Missy, wipe off her slate when she was done forming letters, and suffer as a punching bag for Missus when she directed her frustration over her daughter's slow progress at the lifelong nursemaid.

But as Missy learned, so did Lonely One. Because of Cook's whispered warnings, she knew to keep her face entirely blank during lessons, feigning boredom and perhaps even stupidity so that she might be allowed to keep learning.

"THE WHITE FOLKS DIDN'T 'LOW US TO LOOK AT A BOOK"

If they happened to be a slave on the plantation that could just read a little, they would get rid of him right now. He would ruin the [others]; they would get too smart. (Monroe Brackins, Texas)[20]

The white folks didn't 'low us to look at a book. They would scold us sometimes, whoop us iffen they caught us with our head in a book. (Mary Ella Grandberry, Alabama)[21]

Laws, you better not be caught with a book in your hand. If you did, you were sold. They didn't 'low that. (Louisa Adams, North Carolina)[22]

On her rare forays into the slave quarters, Lonely One had heard whispers of slaves getting limbs cut off for daring to hold a book. She never thought it was a chance she would be willing to take.

But there was magic in those pages.

Lonely One had heard stories, certainly. Every colored child knew about Br'er Fox and Br'er Bear and all the mischief they got into. But until now, she hadn't realized what it meant for a story to be in a book, written in words she could pick up and understand for herself.

Missy paged through the blue-black speller as if it were an odious thing, whining and sighing and acting as though her mother were torturing her. Lonely One looked over her shoulder and saw a host of lines and squiggles turning into words and stories.

She practiced three-letter words in the flour when Cook turned her back. She snuck into the nursery and flipped through a book of nursery rhymes when Missus took Missy into town to pick out fabric for a new frock. She tasted brand-new words in her mouth, forming them on reverent lips.

> I'm glad slavery is over 'cause the Bible don't say nothin' bout it been' right. (Dora Franks, Mississippi)[23]

Lonely One found a few precious moments each day to read the huge family Bible in the parlor. She didn't understand most of its words, but she felt that her mother—whom she could barely remember now—would have wanted her to read them. She would sneak into the parlor while Missus and Missy were in town, when Marse was away on business trips, and any time she was able to finish her long list of chores with enough time to spare to avoid getting caught.

Cook worried, but Lonely One couldn't stop reading that Bible. It wasn't because of religious fervor. Lonely One knew about the secret meetings the others had in brush arbors, shouting and praising the Lord under the cover of darkness and overturned pots. But she had never yet felt that fervor rising in her chest. The closest thing to it was the alchemy of turning those foreign dots and squiggles into words and then turning those words into stories.

Lonely One wished she could write Mama a letter.

COLLECTIVE WITNESS: LETTERS TO MY FRIENDS

Adeline Blakely was full of regret when she told WPA interviewer Mary D. Eugene about her own educational history. Speaking of her enslaver, she shared:

> Mrs. Blakely taught her children at home. Her teaching was almost all they had before they entered the University. When I was little I wanted to learn, learn all I could, but there was a law against teaching a slave to read and write. One woman—she was from the North—did it anyway. But when folks can read and write its going to be found out. It was made pretty hard for that woman. (Adeline Blakely, Arkansas)[24]

There were occasional stories of the enslaved receiving what James Singleton would call a *stolen education*:

> My pappy, he had a stolen education—that was 'cause his mistress back in South Carolina helped him learn to read and write before he left there. You see, in them days, it was against the law for slaves to read. (James Singleton, Mississippi)[25]

Stories of stolen educations were not unheard of, but the threat of punishment and sale was enough to keep widespread illiteracy the norm for the formerly enslaved.

Adeline's wish to write letters to her friends was an opportunity the formerly enslaved rarely participated in, but it was not unknown. Even under the threat of inviting danger, letters were sent back and forth from enslaved family members to free ones, and from those who had run away to those who had been left behind.

On October 27, 1840, Sargy Brown wrote to her free husband in fear of an impending sale:

> This is the third letter I have written you, and have not received any from you; and don't know the reason that I have not re-

ceived any from you. I think very hard of it. The trader has been here three times to look at me. I wish that you would try to see if you can get any one to buy me up there. If you don't come down here this Sunday, perhaps you won't see me anymore. Give my love to them all, and tell them all that perhaps I shan't see you any more. Give my love to your mother in particular, and to Mammy Wines, and to Aunt Betsy, and all the children; tell Jane and Mother they must come down a fortnight before Christmas. I wish to see you all, but I expect I never shall see you all—never no more.[26]

On October 8, 1852, Marie Perkins penned a similar letter to her husband:

> I write you a letter to let you know of my distress. My master has sold Albert to a trader on Monday court day and myself and other child is for sale also and I want you to let [me] hear from you very soon before next court if you can. I don't know when. I don't want you to wait till Christmas.[27]

Her desperation was shared by James Phillips, who had written his wife that same year:

> I will now write to inform you where I am and my health. I am well, and I am in hope that when you receive this, it may find you well also. I am now in a trader's hands, by the name of Mr. Branton, and he is going to start South with a lot of Negroes in August. I do not like this country at all, and had almost rather die than go South. Tell all of the people that if they can do anything for me, now is the time. I can be bought for $900.[28]

In 1854, Stephen Penbroke wrote abolitionist and formerly enslaved pastor James W. C. Pennington:

> Act promptly, as I will have to be sold South. My two sons were sold to the drivers. I am confined to my room with irons on.[29]

So many letters were penned in desperation from those on the precipice of being separated from their families forever. Many of these were published in antislavery journals as proof of the barbarism of the South's "peculiar institution." Some of their authors went on to write narratives that were used as proof of the same.

Memory's Scars

When the WPA set out to interview almost three thousand formerly enslaved Americans in the 1930s, the majority of people they spoke to did *not* have the ear of antislavery publications or activists while they were in bondage. There were no letters to point back to, no paper trail of owning and trading in their trafficked flesh. They spoke from long-past memories of things that would have been lost to the following generations had their words not been captured by the listening ears of the interviewers.

There are plenty of places where the interviewers, the fickle nature of memory, and the politics of the day get in the way of understanding these narratives to the fullest, but as was the case with Henrietta King, the truth was sometimes written not in pen and ink but in the physical scars left by the abuses of slavery.

The emotional and spiritual scars would have been less apparent to the majority white interviewers who took on the task of relating these stories, but they're not invisible. Sallie Crane was another formerly enslaved woman who had physical scars to show interviewer Samuel S. Taylor:

> I have worn a buck and gag in my mouth for three days for trying to run away. I couldn't eat nor drink—couldn't even catch the slobber that fell from my mouth and run down my chest till the flies settled on it and blowed it. 'Scuse me but jus' look at these places. (She pulled open her waist and showed scars where the maggots had eaten in—ed.)

Sallie was running from a type of labor that seemed an impossible task for one who had been so young (seven or eight years old) when it was given: childcare.

> They had so many babies 'round there I couldn't keep up with all of them. I was jus' a young girl and I couldn't keep track of all them children. While I was turned to one, the other would get off. When I looked for that one, another would be gone. Then they would whip me all day for it.

Sallie would grow up to raise eighteen children of her own and be brought low by the Great Depression and other woes of life by the time Samuel met her. A rare Black interviewer, he set her at ease:

> You just come in any time; I can't talk to you like I would a woman; but I guess you can understand me. (Sallie Crane, Arkansas)[30]

The old woman knew what it was to be an isolated caretaker in the Big House, knew what it was to be separated from seventeen children and her parents, to be young enough to still need care but called upon to care for others. She knew what it was to be a Lonely One.

Now at least ninety years old, Sallie didn't know for sure where any of her children were or whether any were alive, save for two of her daughters. Her health was poor, but her memory was still sharp enough to remind her of all she had suffered in her long life.

For a few hours chatting with Samuel, she wasn't alone anymore.

INTERLUDE

Cornelia[1]

Most slave schedules do not take note of the names of the enslaved.

The slave schedule's purpose was to inform the powers that be of how many enslaved people resided in each state. The individual identities and details of the enslaved were of no importance. They are described by their sex, age, and color in those official records. Other details, like names and familial connections, are left up to individual imaginations and sleuthing skills to determine.

In 1860, Joseph McKay Vaden reported holding five people in bondage in the state of North Carolina—one thirty-five-year-old female; three males ages twenty-two, twelve, and twelve; and one female who was ten years old.

In 1937, Cornelia Andrews gave one name and one relationship to that seven-decade-old anonymous slave schedule: the thirty-five-year-old woman was likely her mother, and the ten-year-old little girl was Cornelia herself.

When Cornelia welcomed interviewer Mary A. Hicks into her home on May 21, 1937, the eighty-seven-year-old did not seem the type to demure from difficult questions. In some interviews, the subjects are cagey, veiling their complaints against enslavement by saying *their* masters were quite kind, but the master across the street wasn't as nice; that *they* had plenty of food to eat but they knew the slaves next door often went hungry. Keen eyes can quickly dispel these attempts at obfuscation, which were normally made to white interviewers who lived in small enough towns to know these former masters personally.

But Cornelia didn't talk of *other* masters. In fact, she gave a name to the master who had harmed her in her youth: Doctor McKay Vaden. "He was not good to us," she said, in what one imagines was a solemn tone. *How* he was not good, Cornelia was all too quick to point out: "We had plank houses, but we ain't had much food and clothes. . . . We ain't had much fun. . . . While I could remember they'd sell the mammies away from the babies, and there wasn't no cryin' 'bout it were the master would know 'bout it neither. Why? Well, they'd get beat black and blue, that's why."

Mary Hicks stopped here to ask Cornelia if she'd ever been badly beaten.

"Was I ever beat bad?" Cornelia responded. "No, ma'am, I wasn't."

If Cornelia had been alone in her living room that day, the interview might have ended there. Mary would have asked a few more follow-up questions, convinced that this talkative older woman had told all. Mary's interviews are among North Carolina's shortest, and Cornelia seems to have already exceeded her average talk time.

But Cornelia wasn't alone. She was no longer the anonymous child on the slave schedule: "Female, 10, Black." She had a name. She had a daughter of her own.

Mary doesn't bother naming the daughter in the transcript, but her resoluteness is palpable in Mary's description: "Here the daughter, a graduate of Cornell University, who was in the room listening came forward. 'Open your shirt, mammy, and let the lady judge for herself.'"

Cornelia's eyes flashed, and she sat upright, motionless, as her daughter helped her get her shirt over her head. Her shoulders "were marked as though branded with a plaited cowhide whip."

"I was whooped in public," she said, voice flat. "For breaking dishes and being slow."

Mary Hicks was not conducting the interview alone, and her friend piped up after this revelation: "That must have been horrible, to say the least."

It might have been a sincere interjection trying at sympathy, but Cornelia was upset now. "You don't know nothin," she said. And then she enumerated on more of the violence she had seen and heard of: Alex Heath, beat to death for stealing. Uncle Daniel Sanders, beat and jailed.

And, if Mary's record proves accurate, Cornelia's daughter did not pipe up again.

How many times had the little girl watched her mother dress for the day and seen the scars that marred her back? Had Cornelia ever told this story before? Or was this moment *finally* her daughter's chance to hear the story that Cornelia had always refused to talk about? What sacrifices had Cornelia made to go from being born in slavery to having a daughter graduate from an Ivy League school—one that had only seen its first Black graduate thirty years before?[2]

Sometimes the WPA Narratives meander into life after the Civil War, into marriage, children, schooling, work, and voting records. So many formerly enslaved people were asked for their thoughts on Abraham Lincoln or Franklin D. Roosevelt, on slavery as a practice, pensions, and the state of the world. But if Mary Hicks asked any of these questions, Cornelia's answers did not make it out of the editing process.

What did, however, was the fierceness of a daughter who loved her mother too much to let her lie, who respected her mother's memories too much to let them fade without being recorded for posterity. What made it out was the trauma of Cornelia's reckonings, as deep as the physical scars that crisscrossed her skin.

In interviewing Cornelia Andrews, Mary Hicks uncovered the name that had always belonged to the ten-year-old girl in Dr. Vaden's records. She wasn't born anonymous but was made so through the white supremacist values of the nation that held her in bondage until she was fifteen years old. Her name did not have to be recovered because to the people who knew and loved her, it had never been lost. It had not been accidentally obscured but purposefully left out of the record because the record keepers didn't think it mattered.

It mattered to Cornelia's daughter, though. It mattered as clearly as the scars that marred her mother's back. And Cornelia's little girl was not going to let her story go untold.

There are over three thousand narratives in the WPA records. Cornelia's is one of so many others who were also recorded in ledgers like livestock or consumable products. By saying their names, we are not naming them for the first time but honoring the names that have always belonged to these people whom someone loved.

CHAPTER 3

Lovely

> Master was mighty good to us slaves. He never sent us out to work in the fields till us was most growed-up, say 12 or 14.
>
> Joseph Battle, Georgia

Lonely One wanted nothing more than to move out of the Big House.

She'd had scalding hot water thrown at her. She'd had a slop jar turned over on her head. She'd been shoved, pinched, and verbally browbeaten her entire childhood. And as her long, spindly limbs grew into supple curves, Marse started to notice her, and Missus's wrath grew hotter still.

Lovely

Lonely One was terrified of Marse. Cook bade the young woman to stay out of dodge, to leave whatever room he entered, to do his bidding quickly and efficiently, and most importantly, to not allow him to corner her. She tutted and *tsked* about some of the babies in the fields with their light skin and piercing gray eyes. Eyes like Missy's. Eyes like Marse's.

Cook had a baby like this of her own, her oldest son. The only reason Missus didn't harangue Cook and let her work in the house was because Cook's child was older than Missus and Marse's marriage, and Cook was able to settle down with someone else, bearing only dark-skinned daughters in the interim.

When Lonely One's first blood came, Cook heaved a heavy sigh. "Wish you weren't so lovely," she muttered.

"IFFEN THEY HAD A PRETTY GIRL, THEY WOULD TAKE 'EM"

There were two classes of white folks, some who wouldn't bother with n—— women and others who would; but the ones who wouldn't, wouldn't mix with the ones who would. They would make the women do that. Some of them would treat these children better, and some of them wouldn't. (Mrs. Sutton, Tennessee)[1]

When I was quite a girl I went to a colored person's wedding. She was as black as that thing there (card table top) but she was her young master's woman and he let her marry because he could get her anyhow if he wanted her. (Unnamed Informant, Tennessee)[2]

Iffen they had a pretty girl they would take 'em, and I'se one of 'em, and my oldest child, he boy by Boles, almost white. (Elvira Boles, Texas)[3]

On the plantations, not every one, but some of the slaveholders would have some certain slave women reserved for their own use. (John C. Bectom, North Carolina)[4]

Cook wasn't the only one who noticed her loveliness. As she moved into her teen years, Lonely One became Lovely One. Lovely was allowed greater freedom to roam the plantation, possibly due to Missus catching on to her listening a bit too intently to Missy's lessons. When she walked outside, people noticed her long, slender legs, her graceful neck, and the thick, bountiful coils that Cook helped her wrangle into a long braid.

When Lovely went to her first Christmas dance, several young men and a few long-in-the-tooth ones asked to spin her around the dirt floor in the hollow usually reserved for their illicit church services. They danced her breathless, reveling in the music of her laughter and the gift of every smile. She demurred at their flirtation, shy and unassuming, knowing how beautiful she was but not how to wield that beauty yet.

Talk was that Lovely should be getting married soon and that her mama had been a good breeder. That Marse had bought her explicitly for that purpose. She'd need to live up to the expectation to continue earning her keep.

"THEY WOULD BUY A FINE GIRL AND THEN A FINE MAN"

They would buy a fine girl and then a fine man and just put them together like cattle; they would not stop to marry them. If she was a good breeder, they was proud of her. I was stout and they were saving me for a breeding woman but by the time I was big enough I was free. . . . I'd hear them saying, "She's got a fine shape; she'll make a good breeder," but I didn't know what they were talking about. (Unnamed Informant, Tennessee)[5]

To show you the value of slaves I'll tell you about my grandma. She was sold on the block four times, and every time she brung a thousand dollars. She was valuable 'cause she was strong and could plow day by day, then too she could have twenty children and work right on. (Analiza Foster, North Carolina)[6]

"Behaving" . . . meant living on less food than one should have; mating only at his command and for purposes purely of breeding more and stronger slaves on his plantation for sale. In some cases with women—subjecting to his every demand if they would escape hanging by the wrists for half a day or being beaten with a cowhide whip. (John Henry Kemp, Florida)[7]

Lovely tried to withstand the whispers about her breeding potential. She didn't want to think about marriage or children yet. At no more than fourteen years old and spending most of her time with eight-year-old Missy, she was holding on to her fleeting girlhood. She wanted to play hide-and-seek, search for fairy circles in the woods, and shoot marbles when Missus wasn't around to scold them for such a gentlemanly pastime. She wanted to be a child.

But it was time to put away childish things. By her age, the children of the field hands were joining their parents every day. Other girls her age picked one hundred pounds of cotton a day and faced the painful consequences when their quotas weren't met. Other girls her age had chosen partners for themselves—lest Marse choose one for them—and some already had babies on their hips.

> My mother was born in Mississippi and brought here. My father was born in Maryland. He was an old man when he come here, but they just brought them and put them together. My mother was young—just fifteen or sixteen years old. She had fourteen children and you know that meant a lot of wealth. (Unnamed Informant, Tennessee)[8]

Punishment

Lovely had never expected to get caught in the act of reading. She'd been doing it for several years by now. During the two hours a day when Missy was with her governess and Cook was resting between dinner and supper, Lovely would sneak into the parlor and read.

She'd gone from the Bible to *The Iliad*. At first, she didn't understand the story at all, but over the years she kept returning to the wrath of Achilles, the cunning of Odysseus, the honorable Hector.

Especially Hector.

She'd almost been caught one day as she lost herself crying over Hector and Andromache's last parting:

> Andromache! my soul's far better part,
> Why with untimely sorrows heaves thy heart?
> No hostile hand can antedate my doom,
> Till fate condemns me to the silent tomb.[9]

She had turned those words over and over in her head: "my soul's far better part." Her parents were a hazy memory by now, but she wondered if her father had felt that way about her mother. They'd only been able to see one another twice a week, but he'd always come faithfully, always smiling, always warm.

How had he looked the week he realized Lovely was gone forever?

> My uncle was married but he was owned by one master and his wife was owned by another. He was allowed to visit his wife on Wednesday and Saturday, that's the onliest time he could get off. He went on Wednesday and when he went back on Saturday his wife had been bought by a speculator and he never knew where she was. (Julia Brown, Georgia)[10]

Missus caught her one day, mulling over Homer's words and warring with her own fate. There was nothing for Lovely to do but stand there like a cornered rabbit, chest heaving with panicked breaths she couldn't still. Missus looked almost as gleeful as she did angry: now she had reason to give Lovely the worst punishment in her arsenal.

Lovely was terrified. For all her abuse, she'd never been whipped. She still remembered her mother's scars, the unfurling of the overseer's whip that day Mama had cried out to her for the last time.

Missus grabbed her by the arm and dragged her out the front door and toward the fields where the overseer rode his horse, heckling the souls bent double over cotton to move faster, using his eagle eyes to pick out those he'd make an example of.

"THE OVERSEER WAS PRETTY ROUGH ON US"

Shep Miller was my master. His ol' father, he was a tough one. Lord! I've seen 'im kill 'em. He'd git the meanest overseers to put over 'em. (Elizabeth Sparks, Virginia)[11]

We had white overseers on the plantation, they worked hard producing rice on a very large scale, and late and early. I know they were severely punished, especially for not producing the amount of work assigned them or for things that the overseers thought they should be punished for. (James Calhart, Maryland)[12]

The overseer was pretty rough on us. He want all of us to stay right in line and chop along and keep up with the lead man. If us didn't it [was] the bullwhip. He ride up and down and hit us over the back if us don't do the job right. Sometimes he'd get off he horse and have two slaves hold one down and give him the bullwhip. He'd give it to him too. (John Walton, Texas)[13]

Lovely became the example that day. Missus told the overseer what she had done, and his eyes lit up the same way hers had. It was only after he'd tied Lovely to a tree and ripped out the flimsy back of her dress that she was able to identify the look: bloodlust.

They forced everyone to gather around and watch, from the oldest granny in the children's house to their youngest charge. They wanted everyone to know the penalty for daring to pursue literacy. Missus was convinced that Lovely could not even decipher the words she'd been looking at, but Lovely's desire to understand them was guilt enough for punishment.

Lovely's lips trembled, sobs climbing up her throat in anticipation of the pain.

Missus halted the overseer before the first lick could fall. For a moment, Lovely thought that, perhaps, for love of her daughter, Missus had chosen to spare Lovely from this pain. When she looked up, she saw instead that Missus held a huge pair of sheers. She took Lovely's luscious braid in her hand and lopped it off to the nape of Lovely's neck. Holding the thick plait aloft in triumph, she said, "There. That'll make it easier for you to do the whipping," and walked off.

> The folks said Old Miss was jealous of [Grandma] and Old Master. . . . Old Miss she was might fractious. One day she whipped my grandma and then had her hair cut off. From that on my grandma had to wear her hair shaved to the scalp. (James Brittain, Mississippi)[14]

Later, both acts would linger in Lovely's memory: the whipping and the humiliation of having her head shorn in front of the entire plantation.

"BEAT WOMEN! WHY SURE—BEAT WOMEN JUST LIKE MEN"

I been whipped from sunup till sundown. Off and on, you know. They whip me till they got tired and then they go and res' and come out and start again. They kept a bowl filled with vinegar and salt and pepper settin' nearby, and when they had whipped me till the blood come, they would take the mop and sponge the cuts with this stuff so that they would hurt more. They would whip me with the cowhide part of the time and with birch sprouts the other part. There were splinters long as my finger left in my back. (Sallie Crane, Arkansas)[15]

When she would get mad at one of her slave women, she would make the men tie her down, and she had what they called cat-o'-nine-tails, and after she got the blood to come, she would dip it in salt and pepper and whip her again. Oh, she was mean! (Julia Blanks, Texas)[16]

Massa tied they hands to they feet and tied them to a tree and hit 'bout twenty-five or fifty licks with a rawhide belt. Hide and blood flew then. Next mornin' he'd turn them loose and they'd have to work all day without nothin' to eat. (Louis Cain, Texas)[17]

> Beat women! Why sure he beat women. Beat women just like men. Beat women naked an' wash 'em down in brine. (Elizabeth Sparks, Virginia)[18]

Banished

Lovely woke up in Cook's cabin after the whipping, her flesh flayed, her face swollen from sobbing. The older woman soothed her, applying a salve to her wounds and singing a song Lovely's mother used to sing:

> No more driver's lash for me
> No more, no more
> No more auction block for me
> Many thousands gone

Cook told the young woman she'd been banished from the Big House. "And good riddance," the older woman said. Marse's arms were long, but he usually left women alone once Missus's wrath had rained down on them in its fullest force.

It took several days for Lovely to heal enough to get up and move around. Cook told her that Missus had intended for Lovely to be working in the fields the very next day, but that Missy had begged her mother to let Lovely convalesce for a few days.

"She's not your friend," Cook said, "but that's the very least she could have done."

Lovely would live with Cook. And, in that way, her banishment became the welcome she had longed for. Each night before they went to bed, Cook would teach her how to quilt. Cook offered to use Lovely's little piece of fabric in a quilt just for her, but Lovely wasn't ready to let go of it yet.

To keep things proper, Cook's son moved into another cabin, leaving Lovely with a gaggle of Cook's daughters for company on most of those quilting evenings.

Son was a handsome, dimpled boy several years older than Lovely. He was full of easy smiles and silly jokes, always coming around to cheer her up while she was healing. He brought her a bouquet of wildflowers one day and a petrified beetle shell the next. He asked her about the words she'd learned in the Big House and confessed he'd always wanted to read. And in the scant moments between the end of a work day and Son heading off to his cabin to sleep, Lovely sometimes told him stories from *The Iliad* about Hector and Achilles and Patroclus and Helen of Troy.

And Son told her that she was probably beautiful enough to launch a thousand ships too.

And Cook swatted Son and told him to stop talking that fool talk and get on to bed.

COLLECTIVE WITNESS: COUPLING

Sam and Norfolk were young when their enslaver, "Big Jim" McClain, forced their coupling. When the young couple and their two sons were emancipated in 1865, they were only fifteen and nineteen years old, respectively.

Sam, the younger of the two, was just a boy living with his parents, Peter and Betsey Everett. When they weren't toiling in McClain's fields, they were tending to their vegetable garden, living in constant fear that Big Jim would take their meager harvest for himself as he so often did.

Norfolk, named for Norfolk, Virginia, where she and Sam were enslaved, was older and alone in the world after having been sold away from her parents at a very early age. Everyone called her Nor.

Big Jim was a cruel trafficker in human flesh and known for two things: brutal punishments and breeding. Often he would whip his slaves into insensibility for minor offenses, hanging them by their thumbs whenever they were caught trying to run away.

His breeding devices were also notorious:

> On this plantation were more than 100 slaves who were mated indiscriminately and without any regard for family unions. If their master thought that a certain man and woman might have strong, healthy offspring, he forced them to have sexual relation, even though they were married to other slaves. If there seemed to be any slight reluctance on the part of either of the unfortunate ones, "Big Jim" would make them consummate this relationship in his presence. He used the same procedure if he thought a certain couple was not producing children fast enough. He enjoyed these orgies very much and often entertained his friends in this manner; quite often he and his guests would engage in these debaucheries, choosing for themselves the prettiest of the young women. Sometimes they forced the unhappy husbands and lovers of their victims to look on. (Sam and Louisa Everett, Florida)[19]

Big Jim was far from the only enslaver who coupled up young people to try to increase strong offspring on his plantation.

Elige Davison remembered:

> I been marry once before freedom, with home wedding. Massa, he bring some more women to see me. He wouldn't let me have just one woman. (Elige Davison, Texas)[20]

Jeptha Choice recalled:

> The master was mighty careful about raising healthy families and used us strong, healthy young bucks to stand the healthy gals. When I was young they took care not to strain me and I was as handsome as a speckled pup and was in demand for breedin'. Later on we was 'lowed to marry and the master and missus would fix [us] up and have the doin's in the big house. (Jeptha Choice, Texas)[21]

Several of those interviewed by the WPA remembered that their enslavers specialized in raising children to sell. But very few recall voyeurism to the extent of Big Jim's.

Norfolk and Sam were subjected to this treatment when it came time for their coupling. Norfolk remembered:

> Marse Jim called me and Sam to him and ordered Sam to pull off his shirt—that was all the McClain n—— wore—and he said to me: "Nor, do you think you can stand this big n——?" He had that old bullwhip flung acrost his shoulder, and Lawd, that man could hit so hard! So I jes said "Yassur, I guess so," and tried to hide my face so I couldn't see Sam's nakedness, but he made me look at him anyhow.
>
> Well, he told us what we must get busy and do in his presence, and we had to do it. After that we were considered man and wife. Me and Sam was a healthy pair and had fine, big babies, so I never had another man forced on me, thank God. Sam was kind to me and I learnt to love him.[22]

The couple was still married over seventy years later. They endured enslavement together, as well as the period after emancipation when Big Jim was so hellbent on refusing their freedom that Union soldiers had to come and personally emancipate his plantation.

When Sam and Norfolk were interviewed for the WPA Narratives, they were eighty-six and ninety years old. They lived in Mulberry, Florida, just an hour's drive south of Orlando. By this time in their lives, they were living closer to the opening of Disney World in the 1970s than the end of slavery in the 1860s.

But field worker Pearl Randolph, a member of Florida's Negro Unit (the Black interviewers of that state), observed that the couple had "weathered together some of the worst experiences of slavery, and as they look back over the years, can relate these experiences as clearly as if they had happened only yesterday."

These revelations did not come without coaxing.

In freedom, Norfolk chose the name Louisa. She would no longer go by the name of the place where she had been held in bondage—she would forge a new identity apart from it. She and Sam were living with their youngest son at the time of the 1936 interview, and both were described as "pitifully infirm." But both vividly remembered "the horrors they experienced under very cruel owners" and "it was with difficulty that they were prevailed upon to relate some of the gruesome details recorded here."[23]

Well into their elderly years, Sam and Louisa remembered the humiliation and violation of this first sexual encounter with one another. They still struggled to share the details with an interviewer and with posterity.

Was their youngest son, Sampson, in the room while they talked to Pearl? Did he witness his parents' trauma as they told her? Had they ever told him the exact details of how their union, which had lasted the length of a generous lifetime, had come to be?

Sometimes these questions are answered for us in the narratives. Sometimes we see the children of the formerly enslaved interacting with interviewers, shielding their parents or comforting them. In this narrative, however, we are left to wonder if Sam and Louisa's solace came only from each other in this moment.

Sam was kind to me, and I learned to love him.

That love built a life for them together.

After the war, Sam and Louisa sharecropped until their sons, Elder Peter James, Mitchell, and Sampson, were old enough to help them farm. A Georgia property tax digest shows that by 1890, Sam owned one hundred acres of land and property amounting to $140. Louisa is listed as "keeping house" in the 1880 census. While all three of their children went to school, Sam and Louisa never learned to read or write.

They had weathered so many storms of life together, from the brutal and often unending cycle of sharecropping to land ownership; from their son Elder going off to fight in the Spanish-American War to his death stateside—all starting with the trauma at the beginning of their union together.[24]

Who's Gonna Be Your Man?

Well . . . it's O Lordy me
And it's O Lordy my,
Yes, it's O Lordy me
And it's O Lordy my,
Who's gonna be your man?
Who's gonna shoe your pretty little foot?
Who's gonna glove your hand?
Who's gonna kiss your red ruby lips?
Who's gonna be your man?

It was one of the songs the young women sang while they worked in the loom house, carding and spinning after the cotton had been harvested. While Lovely never acclimated to the work of a harvest, she was a beautiful spinner, and even Missus had to relent in her ire to say so.

So many of their little songs touched on the nature of love:

I come for to see you,
I come for to sing,
I come for to show you,
My little diamond ring. (repeat)
My ring shines like silver,
My ring shines like gold.
Gonna give it to my little Cindy Jane
Hers for to hold
Hers for to hold.

Lovely hadn't known them at first, hadn't been raised around their melodies or the way the other young ladies kept time with tapping feet or well-placed hums. But she learned the songs quickly, singing along with a smile while they teased one another, asking, "Who's gonna hold your hand?"

Lovely knew there'd be no diamond rings. On some plantations, there was no ceremony at all. A master would simply pick a young woman and a young man he thought would bear fine children and put them together with just his word to bind them.

"THEY WASN'T ALLOWED TO MARRY"

They wasn't allowed to marry cause they could be sold and it wasn't no use, but you could lie with 'em. (John Barker, Texas)[25]

In slavery white folks just put you together. Just tell you to go on and go to bed with her or him. You had to stay with them whether you wanted them or not. (Tom Douglas, Arkansas)[26]

No, not any weddings. It was kinder that way. There was a good n—— man and a good n—— woman, and the master would say, "I know you both good n——s and I want you to be man and wife this year and raise little n——s; then I won't have to buy them." (Jim Allen, Mississippi)[27]

On this plantation, young couples jumped the broom. Sometimes they'd even have a party afterward, along with dancing and perhaps a few extra rations some of the women had stored from their gardens. Marriage meant celebration, if not always love.

"YOU HAD TO JUMP OVER A BROOM THREE TIMES"

Most folks them days got married by laying a broom on the floor an jumpin' over it. That seals the marriage, and at the same time brings 'em good luck. (Josephine Anderson, Florida)[28]

When you married, you had to jump over a broom three times. That was the license. If master seen two slaves together too much he would marry them. It didn't make no difference if you weren't but fourteen years old. (Georgina Giwbs, Virginia)[29]

After old man Glass bought Jennie, he held up a broom and they would have to jump over it backwards and then old man Glass pronounced them man and wife. (Will Glass, Arkansas)[30]

Most of the girls knew they had better pick themselves a match before Marse picked a match for them. Their desires would not come into the equation. It was merely a matter of whether they and their future mate seemed to be of strong stock. In fact, sometimes, they were married to strangers from neighboring plantations after an agreement had been struck by their enslavers.

"THEY RAISED CHILDREN TO MAKE MONEY ON JUST LIKE WE RAISE PIGS TO SELL"

Two informants remembered the true value of marriage or coupling in an enslaver's eyes: producing more children. Strong, healthy children were a boon to enslavers, who owned both mother and any child she would bear—in perpetuity.

During slavery if one marster had a big boy and another had a big gal the marsters made them live together. If the woman didn't have any children, she was put on the block and sold and another woman bought. You see, they raised children to make money on just like we raise pigs to sell. (Sylvia Watkins, Tennessee)[31]

In 1861, when he was sixteen years old, Ambrose Willard Douglass was given a sound beating by his North Carolina master because he attempted to refuse the mate that had been given to him—with the instructions to produce a healthy boy-child by her—and a long argument on the value of having good, strong, healthy children. (Ambrose Douglass, Florida)[32]

Lovely knew that she would be under immense pressure to bear Marse a lot of children, as her mother had borne her last master. Cook had explained to her how babies were made, and she'd seen a couple of them born. Even so, she wasn't sure she wanted to be a mother.

To Lovely, motherhood was encapsulated by her last look at her own mother—the older woman kneeling in the dirt, face streaked with tears, keening, howling, arms outstretched and empty hands grasping, while the overseer unfurled his bullwhip to punish her desperation with the lash.

She talked about this with the other girls, and they sympathized with her. But they also warned her not to wait too long to pick, lest she be married off to someone twice her age.

COLLECTIVE WITNESS: ARNOLD'S STORY

The tiny boat was shrouded in inky darkness as the strong current ushered the vessel toward the opposite shore. Two young people sat inside—male conductor and female passenger quieter than the night around them. Neither spoke as the passenger shivered with cold, tensing at every sound, while the conductor rowed as swiftly and quietly as he could. The mile between the Kentucky shore and the Ohio shore seemed to stretch an eternity.

> I know it was a long time rowin' there in the cold and worryin'. But it was short, too, 'cause as soon as I did get on the other side the big-eyed, brown-skin girl would be gone.

When Arnold Gragston recounted this perilous journey, the first of three hundred he would make with other brown-skinned fugitives in his little boat, that big-eyed girl featured heavily in convincing him to make that first trip. He'd just been out to go courting, a ritual so many other young people of his time participated in. Perhaps he'd fantasized about a couple of dances, some hand-holding, a few stolen kisses. He could not have known on his way to talk to that beautiful girl that he was altering the trajectory of his life not toward matrimony but toward freedom.

She didn't say anything. Arnold never even knew her name. But when an old woman told him she had a real pretty girl there who wanted to go across the river, he looked straight at that pretty little thing—brown-skinned and rosy-cheeked with big eyes. Those eyes haunted his dreams that night as he considered whether he'd go back to rescue her the next day:

> All the next day I kept seeing Mr. Tabb laying rawhide across my back, or shootin' me, and kept seeing that scared little brown girl back at the house, looking at me with her big eyes and asking me if I wouldn't just row her across to Ripley. Me and Mr. Tabb lost, and soon as dust settled that night, I was at the old lady's house.

Arnold was a young man then, just beginning to go courting at other Kentucky plantations in Mason County. In the slave state of Kentucky, Arnold's marriage held the potential for more capital for whichever enslaver owned Arnold's wife, because every child she bore would become another piece of property added to the wealth of her enslaver.

Arnold's courtship and marriage was supposed to enrich the slaveholders of Mason County. Whomever he chose, Mr. Tabb would try to purchase for himself and thereby ensure ownership of any offspring produced by the marriage. His courtship should have boasted the promise of an increase of enslaved bodies in Mason County, not a decrease.

And yet, Arnold instead ferried fugitives across the short stretch of the Ohio River to a small town called Ripley, where Presbyterian minister and Underground Railroad conductor John Rankin waited to push them even further to freedom.

Rankin had thirteen children. Had his wife been a Black woman instead of a white one, this increase would have signaled lots of wealth for an enslaver. Yet just one narrow stretch of river over, because of the whiteness the law favored, Mr. and Mrs. Rankin's children were American citizens whose existence was a richness all its own, not counted in the dollars and cents of chattel slavery.

Arnold himself would get to raise his children free as well. Just before the Civil War, he and his young wife made their way first to Ripley, then to Detroit. They had ten children of their own and thirty-one grandchildren.

> The bigger ones don't care so much about hearin' it now, but the Little Bits never get tired of hearin' how their grandpa brought emancipation to loads of slaves he could touch and feel, but never could see.[33]

Arnold might have had a love story with the "scared little brown girl" with big eyes who mesmerized him enough to hazard an illicit journey across the Ohio River. Perhaps, instead of ferrying her to freedom, the two of them could have jumped the broom and borne a passel of children. Perhaps, instead of stealing her away in the night, he could have stolen her chance of freedom with more and more children.

Women accounted for only 19 percent of runaways between 1848 and 1860, likely because the majority of them were mothers.[34] It was hard to hazard the journey North with children in tow. Had Arnold settled down with the big-eyed girl, perhaps they would have eventually escaped together, as Arnold did with his future wife and children. But would Arnold have even become a conductor on the Underground Railroad without the influence of that first pretty face to help him over the fear of punishment from Mr. Tabb?

History will never tell that story. Instead, it will tell the story of a young couple who might have been something more but who chose instead to walk through a different gateway: the girl toward immediate freedom on the other side of the Ohio River, and Arnold into a conductor for the freedom of as many as three hundred others.

Because of his choice, whatever children were born to that pretty girl were born in freedom. She was a Helen of Troy in miniature, her Lovely face launching one ship across one river hundreds of times, turning Arnold Gragston into a ferryman for freedom.

CHAPTER FOUR

Cherished

> Courting them days was like everything I reckon you all do nowadays. You promise to obey the man but before you finish its cussing. Honey. In the olden days husbands loved.
>
> Della Harris, Virginia

In time, Lovely made a choice that surprised no one: she married Son, Cook's boy.

They gathered in the brush arbor one Sunday afternoon with the rest of the plantation folk, minus Marse, Missus, and Missy. They had been married in Marse's parlor by a real preacher with an actual license, but out here in the brush arbor was the ceremony just for the quarters. This time, they didn't have a preacher or a Bible, nor did they commit to a long list of vows. Lovely wore the same day dress she always wore, but she had a crown of flowers on top of the hair she would wear shorn close to her scalp for years to come. Son had shaved for the occasion, dimples deeply creased with a wide, brilliant smile.

They grabbed hands before vaulting over the broom and into their new lives together. Then they danced, celebrating rather than dreading everything that was to come.

Lovely, Cherished

Lovely had been cherished by Son for a very long time. He'd bided his time, patiently waiting for her to choose him on her own. They saw each other every morning for breakfast and every evening for supper, both of which they took under Cook's roof together with the rest of her children.

It had felt slow as molasses when it was happening; Cherished accepting his gifts and then breaking his long, meaningful gazes—telling him her *Iliad* story time and again at his request, but never seeking him out. The months had piled on top of each other, stretching into years, while Son waited for Cherished to make a decision for herself rather than arranging their union through his own machinations by going to Marse and telling him he'd picked his bride.

> Well, n——jus' go to the master and tell him that there's a gal over in Cap'n Smith's place that he want for a wife, if she happen to be there. Then the master go to Cap'n Smith and offer to buy her. Maybe he do and maybe he don't. It depend on whether the Cap'n will sell her, and iffen she a good strong, healthy n——. N——was bought mostly like hosses. (Jeptha Choice, Texas)[1]

> As to marriage, when a slave wanted to marry, why he would just ask his master to go over and ask the other master could he take unto himself this certain gal for a wife. Mind you now, all the slaves that master called out of quarters and he'd make them line up, see, stand in a row like soldiers, and the slave man is with his master when this askin' is going on, and he pulls the gal to him he wants; and the master then makes both jump over broom stick and after they does, they is pronounced man and wife, both staying with the same masters (I mean if John marries Sallie, John stays with his old master and Sal with hers, but had privileges, you know, like married folks; and if children were born all of them, no matter how many, belonged to the master where the woman stayed). (Minnie Fulkes, Virginia)[2]

MARRYING A WOMAN FROM ANOTHER PLACE

In *The Slave Community*, John Blassingame writes:

> Many slaves vowed early in life never to marry and face separation from loved ones. If they had to marry, the slave men were practically unanimous in their desire to marry women from another plantation. They did not want to marry a woman from their own and be forced to watch as she was beaten, insulted, raped, overworked, or starved without being able to protect her.[3]

The practice of going to a different plantation to find a bride, as Arnold Gragston did, was quite common.

Time was running out by the time Cherished accepted Son's sweet proposal. She did not yet love him when they married, but she was safe with him, and Cook reminded her that safety had the makings of love if she gave it time. Son maintained his patience even after they leaped over the broom, kissing her chastely on the cheek as they danced to the fiddle.

As the months stretched on, Cherished would feel the bloom of love for Son. In time, he would become her Sun, moon, and stars. She had a family now, which was something she'd longed for ever since the day she'd been separated from her mother, something she'd feared ever since she understood what family meant for a slave, and something she would hold onto with all of her might, for as long as she could.

COLLECTIVE WITNESS: BETHANY'S STORY

Bethany Veney's marriage to her husband Jerry illustrates the complexity of enslaved unions all too well.

During their wedding, Bethany was very particular about the vows she allowed to be spoken:

> I did not want [the minister] to make us promise that we would always be true to each other, forsaking all others, as white people do in their marriage service, because I knew that at any time our masters could compel us to break such a promise.[4]

Bethany's home was nestled in Shenandoah Valley, future home to farmers' markets, wineries, and other tourist destinations centered around Shenandoah National Park. The gorgeous natural beauty of her home was flanked by the Blue Ridge Mountains to the east, a verdant, would-be National Forest to the west, and the Shenandoah River to the north.

At the time, it was a tiny, picturesque town of about five hundred with several mercantile stores and two or three churches. In less than one hundred years from their love story, Bethany's presence there—the presence of both chattel slavery and free Blacks in and around Appalachia—would be swept away to paint this merry slice of Americana as the home of hardworking, salt-of-the-earth, bootstrap-tugging white folks.

But the town that would someday skew idyllic in the eyes of the beholder was, like nearly every other inch of the state of Virginia, touched by the slave trade. In fact, Louis Hughes, a former slave in Virginia, called the state the "mother of slavery." It had been the first state to welcome African slaves to American shores in 1619 and was a bustling hub of the trade throughout American chattel slavery's heyday.

In 1843, it was where Bethany would watch Jerry, whom she'd only been married to for a handful of months, be led along in a coffle. Another fugitive from slavery, Charles Ball, described coffles in his narrative:

> The women were merely tied together with a rope, about the size of a bed cord, which was tied like a halter round the neck of each;

> but the men . . . were very differently caparisoned. A strong iron collar was closely fitted by means of a padlock round each of our necks. A chain of iron, about a hundred feet in length, was passed through the hasp of each padlock, except at the two ends, where the hasps of the padlocks passed through a link of the chain. In addition to this, we were handcuffed in pairs, with iron staples and bolts, with a short chain, about a foot long, uniting the handcuffs and their wearers in pairs.[5]

Later, Bethany would mourn that Jerry "had committed no offense against God or man."[6] Rather, his enslaver had been caught up in his own debts and sold his slaves to pay them off.

"OLD MARSE DRINKED 'EM UP"

The separation of the enslaved from their families was such a common part of life that there were a host of grim euphemisms for the practice. Two such euphemisms were "drank up" and "put him in her pocket."

The first refers to an enslaver whose drinking problem led first to debt and then to the sale of his human property.

> They said Bill Davis drunk up [my] mother and all her children. (Mattie Fannen, Arkansas)[7]

> Mr. Joe Bues drunk [my grandmother] up and they come and got her and took her off. (Malindy Maxwell, Arkansas)[8]

> Before I could remember much, I remember Lee King had a saloon close to Bob Allen's store in Russell County, Alabama, and Marse John Bussey drunk my mammy up. I mean by that, Lee King took her and my brother George for a whiskey debt. Yes, old Marse drinked 'em up. . . . George was just a baby. (Jim Allen, Mississippi)[9]

The second referred to the selling of an enslaved person and the pocketing of the cash from the sale.

He didn't whip them like some owners did, but if they done mean he sold them. They knew dis so they minded him. One day grandpappy sassed Miss Polly White and she told him that if he didn't behave himself that she would put him in her pocket. Grandpappy was a big man an' I asked him how Miss Polly could do that. He said she meant that she would sell him then put the money in her pocket. He never did sass Miss Polly no more. (Sarah Debro, North Carolina)[10]

Miss Neely told my mother that she was going to sell me and put me in her pocket. She told her more than one time. I recollect that. (Henry Doyl, Arkansas)[11]

I had grown up quite large, before I thought any thing about liberty. The fear of being sold South had more influence in inducing me to leave than any other thing. Master used to say, that if we didn't suit him, he would put us in his pocket quick—meaning he would sell us. (William Johnson, Virginia)[12]

Jerry's enslaver might have been a gambler or an alcoholic who drunk Jerry up. But either way, he put Jerry in his pocket.

An Abroad Marriage

Cherished and her Sun pieced together a life.

They were given their own cabin, and Sun built them a bed and a cedar chest to hold their belongings. He woke each day before dawn to go to the fields, and Cherished went to the loom house to spin. They saw each other at lunchtime and in the evenings, exchanging the gossip of each day with one another.

They found topics to laugh about, new ways to tease one another, new ways to love one another. And though they barely saw each other by the light of day, they loved by candlelight in the darkness of each evening and early morning. During Saturday frolics in the brush arbor, they danced together like the newlyweds they were, spinning and laughing with the joy they found in certain moments.

But it wasn't long before talk started floating around the slave quarters about Marse's whiskey debt.

Mothers clung to their children and wives to their husbands while fathers paced anxious lines across the dirt floors of their cabins. This would not be the first time Marse had drunk up a handful of folks, tossing them to speculators like coins on the saloon counter. And it probably wouldn't be the last.

For the second time in her life, Cherished tensed as the speculator made his rounds in the fields.

This time, it was she who fell in the dirt crying as someone she loved was taken away.

It was Cherished who begged and pleaded for the speculator to take her along too, because what reason did she have to stay?

Cherished was left behind as her beloved Sun was tied to the coffle trailing behind the speculator's horses.

It was happening all over again. She had become her mother.

"WHEN THEY SOLD MANY OF THE POOR MOTHERS"

When they sold many of the poor mothers beg the speculators to sell 'em with their husbands, but the speculator only take what he wants. So maybe the poor thing never see her husband again. (W. L. Bost, North Carolina)[13]

Pa was sold away from Ma when I was still a baby. . . . There was seventeen of us children and I can't remember the names of but two of 'em now. (Rachel Adams, Georgia)[14]

Unlike Cherished's separation from her mother, however, Sun was only taken ten miles up the road to a neighboring farm rather than across state lines. Every Wednesday and Saturday night, he was allowed to come and visit Cherished, so long as he returned before sunup Thursday and before sundown Sunday.

Cherished knew some men preferred a marriage like this. Abroad marriages, they were called. If a man lived abroad, he didn't have to watch his wife being beaten while he stood helplessly by. He didn't have to see a lecherous overseer or master forcing his advances upon her without being able to speak up on her behalf. He didn't have to watch his children being sold away.

"THEY SAW EACH OTHER TWICE A WEEK"

My father had to walk seven miles every Saturday night to see my mother, and be back before sunrise Monday. (J. H. Beckwith, Arkansas)[15]

A man didn't get to see his wife except twice a week. That was Wednesday and Saturday night. (Susan Snow, Mississippi)[16]

They didn't get to see one another but twice a week—that was on Wednesday and Saturday nights—till after the war was over. I can remember Daddy coming over to Marie Henry's plantation to see us. (Jasper Battle, Georgia)[17]

I did not want to marry a girl belonging to my own place, because I knew I could not bear to see her ill-treated. (John Anderson, Missouri)[18]

If my wife must be exposed to the insults and licentious passions of wicked slave drivers and overseers; if she must bear the stripes of the lash laid on by an unmerciful tyrant; if this is to be done with impunity, which is frequently done by slave holders and their abettors, heaven forbid that I should be compelled to witness the sight. (Henry Bibb, Kentucky)[19]

> I thus found myself forced to go, although no colored man wishes to live at the house where his wife lives, for he has to endure the continual misery of seeing her flogged and abused, without daring to say a word in her defense. (Moses Grandy, North Carolina)[20]

In living apart from her, Sun was able to escape the constant threat to his masculinity in the form of not being able to protect his young bride. But that escape was bartered for the intimacy of newlyweds who should have been able to live together. He wasn't there to dry her tears after she was mistreated, to hold her after Missus acted the part of the unmerciful tyrant, to speak gently to her of better days. Sun would miss the cries of their first child as Little One was ushered into the world. He would miss the daily rhythms of a life with Cherished. And if she were sold away in his absence, he would have no way of knowing his wife was gone forever.

There was no workaround for the pain of their separation or the weight of their time spent together. This was the life they had been forced into, and these were the conditions under which they had chosen to love each other.

And they kept choosing one another, despite the risk. Cherished swept the dirt floor of the cabin every Wednesday morning in preparation for his evening arrival. She sent him off with extra rations every Sunday night. And Sun never missed a single day of making his way to Cherished, beaming on her doorstep, glistening from the ten-mile walk he'd have to take again all too soon.

COLLECTIVE WITNESS: RISKING LOVE

The enslaved knew when they married that separation was an ever-present threat. But they married anyway. They married because the masters bade it: "[If] people were capital, children were interest."[21]

> The boss man had a white preacher sometimes, and there was plenty good beef cornbread. But if the boss didn't care much, he jus' lined 'em up and said, "Mandy, that's your husband, and Rufus, that's your wife." (James Martin, Texas)[22]

But they also married out of an abiding love for one another. Callie Williams remembered:

> Then master say, join hands and jump the broomstick and you is married. The ceremony wasn't much but they stuck lots closer then, and you didn't hear about so many divorces and such as that. (Callie Williams, Alabama)[23]

Mrs. Della Harris remembered:

> In olden days, the husbands loved. (Della Harris, Virginia)[24]

Despite the risk of separation—so many loved.

A LOVE UNTO DEATH

My grandfather was sold to a man in South Carolina, to work in the rice field. Grandmother drowned herself in the river when she heard that grand-pap was going away. I was told that grand-pap was sold because he got religious and prayed that God would set him and grandma free. (Mary James, Maryland)[25]

A LOVELESS UNION

Marriages between the enslaved were not always born of love. Sixteen-year-old Rose Williams remembered the traumatic event of being paired with a man named Rufus. Their first night together, she kept him from climbing into her bed by waving a fire poker at him.

Her enslaver scolded her for her resistance to the match.

"The next day the master call me and tell me, 'Woman, I's pay big money for you and I's done that for the cause I wants you to raise me children. I's put you to live with Rufus for the purpose. Now, if you doesn't want a whipping at the stake, you do what I want.' I thinks 'bout master buying me off the block and saving me from being separated from my folks and 'bout being whipped at the stake. There it am. What am I to do? So I decides to do as the master wish and so I yields."

Rose had two children with Rufus, but forced him to leave once she was free. She never married again, so scarred was she by her experience.

"After what I does for the master, I's never wants no truck with any man. The Lord forgive this colored woman, but he have to excuse me and look for some others to replenish the earth." (Rose Williams, Texas)[26]

Partus Sequitur Ventrem

Cherished was not allowed to leave with Sun because Marse still hoped she would produce as many offspring as her mother had. And if Sun had been sold farther away than the ten-mile radius, Marse would have paired Cherished with someone else who could sire the type of stock he wanted. Cherished and Sun's match-worthiness would depend upon their ability to bear strong children.

And in time, they did.

Before long, her belly became round with their first baby, and she soon worked each day in the company of reassuring kicks from the little person buried beneath her ribcage. Just like her own mother, and countless women before her, she was afforded neither extra rest nor rations, neither visits from a doctor nor the modesty of confinement. She was expected to complete the same amount of work as always and was liable to the same harsh punishment if she made a mistake.

"THEY'D DIG A HOLE IN THE GROUND"

When women was with child they'd dig a hole in the ground and put their stomach in the hole, and then beat 'em. They'd always whop us. (Anne Clark, Texas)[27]

Some of the overseers were mean men: they wanted slaves to have babies 'cause they was valuable. So when a slave was about to produce a baby and he wanted her whipped, he had a hole dug in the ground and made her lay across it. And her hands and foots were tied, so she had to submit quiet-like to the beating with a strap. (Rebecca Fletcher, Louisiana)[28]

One woman, on a plantation not so far from us, was expecting, and they tied her up under a hack-a-berry tree, and whipped her until she died. Most any time at night if you go 'round that tree, you could hear that baby cry. I expect you could hear it yet. (Mandy McCullough Crosby, Alabama)[29]

Cherished heard that other plantations rewarded women with less work and greater favor with every child they bore. But on her plantation, her labor remained just as vigorous despite the value of her children. Yet still, each night, Cherished stayed up to quilt, the practice making her feel closer to her mother. She wove in bits of Sun where she could—an old shirt, a bit of his breeches, a patch of fabric from the dress she'd worn on her wedding day. She wasn't ready to sew in the piece she'd kept close all of these years, the one that was so faded from handling.

Cherished dreaded the day of her baby's birth. As much as she wanted to hold the child in her arms, she knew the babe was safer in her womb. Once born, the child would no longer be an inseparable part of Cherished. They could be sold away from her as easily as she had been from her mother and Sun from her, simply because their mother was a slave. That would be the condition of every child Cherished bore:

> Whereas some doubts have arisen whether children got by any Englishman upon a Negro woman shall be slave or free, Be it therefore enacted and declared by this present grand assembly, that all children borne in this country shall be held bond or free only according to the condition of the mother—*Partus Sequitur Ventrem*. And that if any Christian shall commit fornication with a Negro man or woman, he or she so offending shall pay double the fines imposed by the former act.
>
> Laws of Virginia, 1662 Act XII; Latin added by William Henig, The Statutes at Large, 1819[30]

By bearing a child, Cherished would bring another slave into the world. Her love for this baby warred with her heartbreak over how the child would exist in a world that considered them property. This baby was the fruit of love between Cherished and Sun, but their love could not prevent their child's identity from being distilled into a line on a ledger.

Sun was joyful, though. His whole face lit up when Cherished told him he would soon be a father. In their stolen moments together, they pretended they could have a free life with their child, one in which they worked together on a little farm with chickens, a couple of cows, and a horse. Sun would work his own land and take his own crops to market. Cherished would cook the food they decided to eat from their stores, not the stingy rations of the overseer. They would save up to add more land, which they'd pass down to their many children.

These were the dreams they shared in the darkness, Sun holding Cherished tight, curved around her back, his free hand rubbing her belly as it stretched and grew. This was the *someday* they built in their imaginations, a future that seemed entirely out of their grasp but one they dared hope for nonetheless.

The questions they dared not ask themselves swirled in the quiet of their unspoken fears.

Even if freedom were imminent, how many more debts would Marse accrue before it arrived? How many more times would Cherished and Sun be parted? How many children would they bear only to lose to the gaping maw of the slave trade? How long could they hold their family together before circumstances ripped it apart? And once ripped, could the breach ever be mended?

COLLECTIVE WITNESS: TEMPIE'S STORY

Tempie Herdon Durham of North Carolina was 103 years old when she reminisced to Travis Jordan about her wedding to Exter Durham. She wore white gloves, a white dress, and a veil made from a white window curtain. She had a wedding cake complete with a tiny bride and groom on top, and mistress "Miss Betsy" played the wedding march on the piano as they stood on the front porch of the Big House to wed. A Black preacher, Uncle Edmond Kirby, married them. Afterward, Master George had them jump over the broom backward "to see which one going to be the boss of your household."

George held the broom a foot off the ground, and Tempie remembered sailing over it with ease while poor Exter's legs got tangled up on the broom and he fell on his face. It was all in good fun, though, and everyone laughed. Exter could only stay for one night since he was owned by a different enslaver, and from then on, he was only able to visit Tempie from Saturday to Sunday night:

> Exter done made me a wedding ring. He made it out of a big red button with his pocket knife. He done cut it so round and polished it so smooth that it looked like a red satin ribbon tied 'round my finger. That sure was a pretty ring. I wore it 'bout fifty years, then it got so thin that I lost it one day in the wash tub when I was washin' clothes.

Tempie remembered that she was worth "a heap" to George because she and Exter had seven big, strong children while they were enslaved:

> Lucy Carter was the only [one] on the plantation that had more children than I had. She had twelve, but her children was sickly and mine was muley strong and healthy. They was never sick.

Tempie's remembrances of slavery were not as brutal as the memories of others. In fact, toward the end of her narrative, she says that slavery was better than freedom because the enslaved were well taken care of. Living in the Jim Crow South at the height of the Great Depression, Tempie looked back fondly on knowing where her meals would come from, having a doctor on call, and having a master and mistress whom she reported as very kind.

Like many of those interviewed by white WPA interviewers, Tempie almost seemed to *miss* her life of bondage and to think fondly of those who enslaved her. However, before waxing so eloquent about the good old days, she betrayed a kernel of a different story:

> I was glad when the war stopped, 'cause then me and Exter could be together all the time instead of Saturday and Sunday.[31]

As kind as she reported her master and mistress to be, they still enforced the separation of a wife from her husband and treated the wife kindly because her children turned a profit. Even with her reports of being taken care of well, Tempie knew she was "worth a heap" because of the number of children she bore George and Betsy Herndon.

The security she spoke of could have so easily been broken by experiencing forced separation from the seven children she bore in bondage.

Tempie and Exter made a home together after the war. At first, they stayed on with Master George and Miss Betsy, renting a little plot of land for a fourth of their earnings. Eventually, they saved up three hundred dollars and bought a small farm of their own. They had a horse, a steer, a cow, two pigs, some chickens, and four geese. And they had two more children "that wasn't born in bondage."

Maggie Bond told Irene Robinson that "the happiest year of my whole life was the first year of my married life." Unlike Tempie, she'd been married after emancipation:

> I hardly had a change of clothes. I had lots of friends. I went to the field with Scott. I pressed cotton with two horses, one going around and the other coming. Scott could go upstairs in the gin and look over at us. We had two young cows. They had to be three years old then before they were any service. I fed hogs. I couldn't cook but I learned. I had been a house girl and nurse. (Maggie Bond, Arkansas)[32]

Maggie hadn't married while in bondage and didn't have to be separated from her husband or their children. They didn't have much, but they made a life together, making do as they found their way through. They loved one another in the simplicity of free farming life.

Surely Tempie could relate. The young woman had gone from seeing her husband only once a week and parenting her children alone to working together to build a home. She had gone from a life where her value was in her lucrative ability to bear children to a life where she and her children faced no risk of separation through buying and selling.

Tempie and Exter's marriage survived long enough for them to love each other in the days of freedom.

It was a privilege not afforded to so many others.

INTERLUDE

Mary[1]

Sarah "Zoe" Posey was the daughter of a Confederate captain.

She was born in December 1867, two years after the Confederate surrender. Named Sarah after her father's mother, she went by Zoe for most of her adult life, the balance of which had been lived long before she knocked on Mary Harris's door in October 1940.

The two women weren't far apart in age, as Mary was eighty-six and Zoe seventy-two, and they were both born and bred in the South—Mary in Louisiana, Zoe in Alabama and Mississippi. Mary was a former slave Zoe was interviewing for the Louisiana Writer's Project.

Zoe had spent much of her life mining a quaint version of Southern history, relying on phrases like "this old mammy of a bygone day," "those antebellum 'aunties' that one seldom sees nowadays," and "the quality born Negro." The latter, she described this way:

> The Negro or colored race is not so divided. But between those "raised in the Big House" on the old plantation, and their descendants, there is an impenetrable gulf. True, the educated Negro has achieved a culture in education and wealth that is far above his raising; but nothing perhaps can give the refinement, the spiritual touch, as was bestowed on the old aunties and uncles of another day.

A month before speaking with Mary, Zoe interviewed Frances Lewis, who struck her as "not embittered or prejudiced." Indeed, Frances had spoken with "love and affection for old mass and old slavery days."

"She admits life was harder than it is now, but that made better men and women," Zoe surmised. Then, almost wistfully, she added: "Truly, we will not see her like again."

When Zoe came to Mary, it was clear she was looking for a story of the old South that she'd grown up hearing her father had risked his life to protect. In Zoe's imagination:

> Slavery was a most unfortunate thing, but that all masters were not cruel. Old slaves still tell of their love for "old Miss" and "old Marse," and the loyalty and love existing between them could never have been created in rancorous hearts.

In contrast to the *not* bitter Frances Lewis, Zoe writes that Mary Harris describes her mother as bitter, and as having been "brutally beaten." She quotes Mary as saying that the cruelest masters were usually foreign-born, not American. "So just set it down when you hear of brutal treatment, that it was foreigners."

Doubtless, Zoe had her own slaveholding father in mind when seeking to exonerate the men who'd participated in the enterprise.

Zoe Posey represented a large percentage of interviewers from the WPA: white, female, and raised by slaveholders. In her hands, the most despicable remembrances of slavery could be softened as portraying the exception to an overall benevolent rule. The stakes for mining quaint stories from the elderly were high for a woman who celebrated her father's legacy. And most of the time, she was able to write her version of events uncontested.

However, when she returned to follow up on the interview, she was faced not with Mary Harris but with the woman's son, whom Zoe described as standing guard outside of the house. When he answered the door, he reportedly said:

> You wish to see my mother? I'm sorry, but I cannot permit her to be interviewed. Slavery! Why are you concerned about such stuff? It's bad enough for it to have existed, and when we can't forget it, there is no need of rehashing it.

Zoe's response is not a direct quote, but she communicated the gist of her intentions:

> We were only trying to preserve from the reminiscences of old people, white and colored, what they remembered or had heard from their parents—old songs, work and spirituals, customs, fables, and things on that order. If they cared to talk about slavery, which most of them did, we were interested in hearing about it, but if they chose to steer clear of it, that was all right.

Why Mary's son mentioned bitterness in his next response is not recorded, but Zoe had a fondness for that word.

"Bitter? Yes, I'm bitter. I have a right to be. My mother tells me about the brutality of those days, how they whipped unmercifully their slaves," he said.

"But every slaveholder was not like that," Zoe responded.

Mary's son retorted:

> Yes'm I'm bitter. And the more I think about it, the madder I get. Look at me. They say I could pass for white. My mother is bright too. And why? Because the man who owned and sold my mother was her father. But that's not all. That man I hate with every fiber of my body. And why? A brute like that, who could sell his own child into unprincipled hands, is a beast. The power—just because he had the power and thirst for money.

This response would have soured any further attempts to spin Mary's story into a benign recollection of bygone days. The idyllic minstrelsy of a "mammy" and "auntie" in a calico dress did not mesh with the vicious image of a slaveholder selling his own daughter to turn a profit.

Apparently, Mary Harris's son then relented and told the interviewers they could speak to his mother, if they still wanted to.

Zoe wasn't interested. She wrote:

> But after such a tirade we were afraid, deciding that discretion was the better part of valor. It was our first experience with a madman!

That is where Mary Harris's story ends.

Zoe Posey has an easily searchable genealogy. Her mother's name was Frances. She had five sisters, Talulah, Hilary, Helen, Maude, and Katherine, and a brother named Benjamin Lane Posey Jr. Zoe died in New Orleans, Louisiana, in 1964 and is buried at Cedar Rest Cemetery.

If Zoe had been interviewing Mary to learn her story rather than garner support for her vision of "the good old days," would the name of Mary's mother be included in these pages? Would her son's name be there? Would they have tried to trace the family tree that branched into lives both enslaved and free, both white and Black?

Would Zoe have stopped to connect the dots between Mary's mother, who had been brutally beaten, and the father of the son who now tried to protect Mary?

What difference would a compassionate interviewer have made in rendering Mary's story—her history—instead of using Mary's story as a prop for her own idyllic view of antebellum days?

If Mary Harris's story is ever recovered, it will be by someone who is looking for her and not for the exoneration of those who enslaved her.

CHAPTER FIVE

Mother

Honey, you ain't going to believe this, but I is the mammy of thirty children. Jesus got 'em counted and so is me.

Molly Ammonds, Alabama

She was stooped in the field when the birth pains started.

Normally she worked at the loom or in the children's house, but during harvest, all hands were on deck. Her aching would not produce offspring for Marse for several more hours, which meant she was expected to haul in just as much cotton today as she'd done yesterday and every other harvest where she *hadn't* been pregnant.

"Steady," whispered a friend, reaching out to help her through another contraction.

The air had a bit of a nip as September ebbed into October. Cherished was Mother now of two little boys who tumbled around in the children's house, giving Granny a run for her money, and of this baby that Granny was convinced would be a little girl:

> Of course you can tell whether a baby is going to be a boy or a girl before it's born. If the mother carries that child more on the left and high up that baby will be a boy and if she carries it more to the middle that will be a girl. (Easter Sudie Campbell, Kentucky)[1]

Mother breathed out heavy, eyes slipping shut as her hand found its way to the sharp, ever-increasing pain in her back. She groaned a bit, shifting from one bare foot to the other, grounding herself in the rich Delta soil before letting out a bellow that shocked everyone around her.

Mother had felt out of control so often in her life—when she was taken from her own mama, when she was harangued by Missus in the Big House, when Sun was sold away from her. And she felt that loss of control now as her body contorted with another contraction. It was a lit match, burning a painful path up her thighs, through her pelvis, around her core, bending her double, half in shock, half in agony.

She was not in control of the sounds she made, low and guttural, or the way her body contorted to shield itself from a pain that was radiating from within.

"I don't think you're going to make it to the end of the row," her friend said, pulling her arm.

Mother swatted her away. "You know he won't let us leave unless the baby is crowning," she muttered.

A furious contraction seized her body, rocketing pain from her abdomen to the back of her knees. She sank into the earth, swaying on hands and knees, moaning, brows knit as she fought through the pain. It felt like a blinding burst of light, and tears sprang to Mother's eyes. She was losing control again.

"I think she's crowning," the friend teased.

> Sickness was negligible—childbirth being practically the only form of a Negro woman's "coming down." (Della Briscoe, Georgia)[2]

Labor brought pain in so many ways. The physical upheaval sent Mother reeling, but it was the emotional upheaval that brought tears to her eyes. Marse was in debt again, selling off any "bits and bobs" he could, and Mother was terrified of being separated from this child. As long as her daughter was within her, the Little One was hers to keep. As soon as she took her first breath of outside air, she belonged to someone else.

Where oh where has my little baby gone?

If she could have crossed her legs and kept that baby girl inside of her until a miraculous emancipation came, she would have. If she could steel herself against the pain, deny labor's demand for her child's entrance into this wretched world, she would.

But Mother was not in control.

Her body betrayed her, doing the work that women's bodies had been doing since the dawn of time: bringing forth new life. Bidden, unbidden, it didn't matter—the baby would be born.

When she roared that little girl into the world—for of course Granny had been right—Mother's cry was also for the uncertain future her children would face. She remembered all too well her separation from her own mother and hoped against hope that she and this Little Bit would never be parted. She prayed that they would remain together, this Little Bit who was both part of her and part of the property of the man who owned her. She prayed that Marse would not sell this child.

Mother dared to hope as she held her child in the quilt she had made while she carried her, rocking her, praying for the first time in her life to ask that she and this sweet babe would stay together.

But it was not to be.

"THEY USED TO SELL THE LITTLE CHILDREN AWAY"

My mother told me that they used to sell the little children away from the breasts of their mothers. (Annie Bridges, Missouri)[3]

'Bout the worst thing that I ever seed, though, was a slave woman at Louisburg who had been sold off from her three weeks old baby, and was being marched to New Orleans. (Josephine Smith, North Carolina)[4]

Aunt Millie cried so much 'cause she had to leave her young baby that they talked of whipping her, but they said "We cannot sell her if we whup her" and so they carried her on. Mother said Master Weldon Edwards sold four women away from their young children at one time. (Roberta Manson, North Carolina)[5]

Once my mother and I were out in the woods picking huckleberries and heard a noise as of someone moaning in pain. We kept going toward the sound and finally came to a little brook. Near the water was a Negro woman with her head bent over to the ground and weeping as if her heart was broken. Upon asking her what had caused her agony she finally managed to control her emotions enough to sob out her story. The Negro woman said then that her master had just sold her to a man that was to take her far away from her present owner and incidentally her children. She said this couldn't be helped but she could ask the good Lord to let her die and get out of the misery she was in. (Mrs. Rhuben Gilbert, Kentucky)[6]

Gone to Heaven

Mother was pregnant again, in time.

Such was the way of things.

One baby was sold, but there would be more. And more. And more, until Mother's heart broke or her body broke, whichever came first.

But this birth wasn't as straightforward as the first three had been. This time, Mother went way past when Granny thought the baby would be due, so Granny had to brew some tansy tea to help get things going:

I was a midwife myself, to black and white, after freedom. The Thomson doctors all liked me and told people to "get Nancy." I used "tansy tea"—heap of little root—made black pepper tea, fetch the pains on 'em. (Nancy Boudry, Georgia)[7]

When the pains did come, they felt as though they'd break Mother in two. Granny put an ax under the bed to help cut the pain, but the labor went on for two days after the first pains had started:

> The granny would put a rusty piece of tin or an ax under the mattress and this would ease the pains. The granny put an ax under my mattress once. This was to cut off the after-pains and it sure did too, honey. (Julia Brown, Georgia)[8]

Sun was at her side the second day, a Wednesday, and refused to leave her on the third day. They all knew there would be consequences for him missing curfew, but they were also afraid Mother was about to die. Granny had never witnessed a labor quite like this in all her years of practicing midwifery. The labor stretched on longer than any she'd seen before.

"HE WOULD OFTEN SLIP BACK TO US"

Two Mississippi narratives tell the story of what happened when fathers visited their families without a pass.

My father was sold away from us when I was small. That was a sad time for us. Mars wouldn't sell the mothers away from their children so us lived with her without the fear of being sold. My pa sure did hate to leave us. He missed us and us longed for him. He would often slip back to us' cottage at night. Us would gather 'round him and crawl up on his lap, tickled slap to death, but he gave us these pleasures at a painful risk. When his Mars missed him he would beat him all the way home. Us could track him the next day by the blood stains. (Hannah Chapman, Mississippi)[9]

My pa and ma wasn't owned by the same masters. My pa was owned by Marse Bill Brown who owned a plantation near Marse Easterlin. And Marse being curious like he wouldn't let pa come to see ma an' us. At night he would slip over to see us and old Marse was most always on the lookout for everything. When he would catch him he would beat him so hard till we could tell which way he went back by the blood. But pa, he would keep coming to see us and take the beatings. (Vinnie Busby, Mississippi)[10]

The twins were born on the third day, one howling, one perfectly still.

Hush little baby,
Don't you cry
You'll be an angel
By and by

Mother did not cry when they told her that her new baby girl had gone to heaven. She was sad—of course she was sad—but she was glad too.

COLLECTIVE WITNESS:
"I WOULD'VE BEEN GLAD TO DIE TOGETHER"

After Bethany Veney lost her husband Jerry forever to the power of the slave trade, she found out she was pregnant with their daughter, Charlotte.

For Bethany, as with so many other Black enslaved women, her motherhood was fraught with fear:

> My dear white lady, in your pleasant home made joyous by the tender love of husband and children all your own, you can never understand the slave mother's emotions as she clasps her newborn child, and knows that a master's word can at any moment take it from her embrace; and when, as was mine, that child is a girl, and from her own experience she sees its almost certain doom is to minister to the unbridled lust of the slave-owner, and feels

> that the law holds over her no protecting arm, it is not strange that, rude and uncultured as I was, I felt all this, and would have been glad if we could have died together there and then.[11]

Bethany was not the only formerly enslaved mother to feel this way about her daughter, struggling with the future she knew the girl would experience.

In January 1856, Margaret and Robert Garner, along with their four children and several other people, stole their enslaver's sled and made the chilly trek across the frozen Ohio River—the same river across which Arnold Gragston ferried hundreds of enslaved refugees from Kentucky to Ohio. The family might have been headed further north still, to Canada, but they were apprehended before they could make it.

Rather than see her daughter returned to slavery, Margaret Garner killed the toddler with a butcher knife. Her other children were also wounded, making it clear that Garner intended to kill all four of them, as well as herself, rather than see them taken back into slavery.

Margaret's gruesome decision shocked the nation, but she was not the first enslaved mother to contemplate death for her children rather than a life of slavery. They held tender lives in their wombs and knew that birth meant all manner of suffering. And sometimes, they tried to stop birth before it even began, chewing cotton root as a form of birth control:

> I remember how mother told me the overseer would come to her when she had a young child and tell her to go home and suckle that thing, and she better be back in the field at work in 15 minutes. Mother said she knew she could not go home and suckle that child and get back in 15 minutes so she would go somewhere and sit down and pray the child would die. (Celia Robinson, North Carolina)[12]

"'RESISTANCE' AND 'ACCOMMODATION'"

Infanticide and abortion are topics both shrouded in mystery when it comes to the lives of the enslaved. As Jennifer L. Morgan posits in *Laboring Women*, we can't diminish an enslaved woman's childbearing as either complete resistance *or* complete compliance.

> Women who became mothers enriched their captors' estates while simultaneously creating the communities that would foster profoundly complicated opposition to and compliance with American racial domination. Women who did not become mothers mourned the loss of their birthright or celebrated this blow to slaveowners' domination. "Resistance" and "accommodation" are static poles at opposite sides of a spectrum whose intent is to capture the wide range of responses to repression but whose effect, I would argue, is quite the opposite. Resorting to a binary view, even if one does so in service of illustrating the range of responses that run along the line between two points, suggests an ability to clearly delineate the meaning of various behaviors and does so while suggesting that there is consensus about the terms in play.[13]

The truth is complicated. Mother's story is just one version of a story that could have been told.

The Little Nurse

Mother was much more vigilant about her newest baby than she had been with her older children. She did not want to leave him in the children's house. Instead, she had one of her older sons help her watch him at the edge of the cotton fields for the rest of the harvest season. She would work a row and meet her baby at the end, suckling him in the autumn chill before laying him back on a blanket and bidding his older brother to watch him well. Her oldest son was barely six, though, and was often found quite wanting in his little duties.

"MAMMY HAD ENOCH BRING ME SO SHE COULD SUCKLE ME"

At this period, my principal occupation was to nurse my little brother whilst my mother worked in the field. Almost all slave children have to do the nursing; the big taking care of the small, who often come poorly off in consequence. I know this was my little brother's case. I used to lay him in the shade, under a tree, sometimes, and go to play, or curl myself up under a hedge, and take a sleep. He would wake me by his screaming, when I would find him covered with ants, or mosquitos, or blistered from the heat of the sun, which having moved round whilst I was asleep, would throw the shadow of the branches in another direction, leaving the poor child quite exposed. (John Brown, Georgia)[14]

Once when I was a baby, my sister was sitting by the fireplace rocking me and she fell asleep and let me fall in the fireplace and I was burned on the hand. Four of my fingers was burned and have never come out straight. (Louis Hamilton, Missouri)[15]

I tell you what I remember. I 'member my mammy had a son named Enoch and he nursed me in slave days when mammy was workin' in the field. They didn't 'low them to go to the house but three times a day—that was the women what had babies. But I was so sickly mammy had Enoch bring me to the fence so she could suckle me. (Becky Hawkins, Arkansas)[16]

Mother often thought about Little Missy's childhood in the Big House—of dolls and dress-up and make-believe. She thought of

Missy's tutor and governess, of Missy's books and toys. When she had worked in the Big House, Mother had been envious of Missy's upbringing for herself, and now she coveted it for her own children.

They made what fun they could, shooting marbles, running down to the creek, playing tag in the yard when dusk fell, but too often they were chided to slow down, to keep quiet, not to draw attention to themselves lest Marse notice a young buck fit for sale or a young filly fit for eventual mating. She tried to make her children invisible, while Missy could grow up being seen.

It wasn't much of a childhood at all.

But then, it wasn't much of a motherhood, either.

COLLECTIVE WITNESS:
"IN THE EVENING, THEIR MAMMIES WENT TO SEE 'EM"

Millie Williams was born in April 1851. She knew this because "Marster Dunn, he was my marster that brought me to Texas, he told me." She didn't know much about the details of her birth outside of her birth month because she was "separated from my folks when I's young."

Though she couldn't remember what county or town she'd been born in, she knew she'd come from Tennessee. Her mother's name was Martha, but she didn't know who her father was because "in slavery, they wasn't no license to marry for the slaves. No sir, they just put 'em together like they do cattle and horses."

When Millie was sold for the first time, it was alongside her mother and infant sister, whose name Millie couldn't quite remember when she was interviewed by Joe W. Colbert in Fort Worth, Texas, in 1937. At eighty-six, Millie's remembrance of her earliest life was spotty, but she did recall bringing her sister out to the field where her mother was working so Martha could nurse the baby.

She also remembered getting in trouble once when her mother left the field to come to the house for water, which Millie gave her, before handing her mother the baby to nurse: "The mistress, she caught my Mother and told her if she ever come in again she would tell the master."[17]

Mothers saw their children at the beginning and end of each day. They were only united during the day when they needed to nurse them, and only if they lived on a plantation without a wet nurse who "freed them up" to work in the fields all day.

Cheney Cross remembered looking after several babies as a child:

> I watched over them children day and night. I washed them and fed them and played with them. One of the babies had to take goat's milk. When she cry, the mistress say, "Cheney, go on and get that goat." Yes Lawd! And that goat show did talk sweet to that baby. Just like it was her own. She look at it and wag her tail so fast and say: "Ma-a-a-a-a." Then she lay down on the floor whilst us holds her feet and let the baby suck the milk. (Cheney Cross, Alabama)[18]

When children like Millie weren't available to watch the babies, the elderly who were beyond working health would take on the task. Jeptha Choice remembered:

> When babies was born old n—— grannies handled them cases, but until they was about three years old, they wasn't 'lowed round the quarters, but was wet nursed by women who didn't work in the field and kept in separate quarters and in the evenin' their mammies went to see 'em. (Jeptha Choice, Texas)[19]

Charlotte Beverly of Texas recalled that her "mistus" enjoyed looking after the enslaved babies, as she had no children of her own. Charlotte said, "I'd blow the horn for the mothers of the little babies to come in from the fields and nurse 'em, in mornin' and afternoon."[20]

As Ank Bishop remembered:

> All the women on Lady Liza's place had to go to the field every day and them what had suckling babies would come in 'bout nine o'

clock in the morning and when the bell ring at twelve and suckle them. One woman tended to all of 'em in one house. Her name was Ellie Larkin, and they called her "Mammy Larkin." She all the time sent me down to the field for to get 'em come suckle the children, 'cause that made it hard on her when they gets hungry and cry. (Ank Bishop, Alabama)[21]

Rebecca Fletcher told interviewer Zoe Posey:

The children were left behind. An old woman had the care of 'em, and it was in a big kitchen where she cooked and fed 'em. That was in slavery times. After Freedom when the mothers worked for theyselves, they took the babies along to the fields, and put a piece of fat meat in a cloth and tied it round like a tit. They put a string to it and fastened it to the big toe, so's if they tried to swallow it their toe would jerk it out. (Rebecca Fletcher, Louisiana)[22]

Sometimes, like Mother, women would set their babies on blankets or in troughs while they worked. Other times, they left their children at home in the care of older siblings or elders. No choice came without risks:

My oldest brother, one older'n me, burned to death. My mother was a field hand. She was at work in the field. When she come to the house, the cabin burned up and the baby burned up too. That grieved her mighty bad. (Henry Doyl Brinkly, Arkansas)[23]

THE DEATH OF SIXTY BABIES

Once on the Blackshear place, they took all the fine looking boys and girls that was thirteen years old or older and put them in a big barn after they had stripped them naked. They used to strip them naked and put them in a big barn every Sunday and leave them there until Monday morning. Out of that came sixty babies.

They was too many babies to leave in the quarters for some one to take care of during the day. When the young mothers went to work Blackshear had them take their babies with them to the field, and it was two or three miles from the house to the field. He didn't want them to lose time walking backward and forward nursing. They built a long old trough like a great long old cradle and put all these babies in it every morning when the mother come out to the field. It was set at the end of the rows under a big old cottonwood tree.

When they were at the other end of the row, all at once a cloud no bigger than a small spot came up, and it grew fast, and it thundered and lightened as if the world were coming to an end, and the rain just came down in great sheets. And when it got so they could go to the other end of the field, that trough was filled with water and every baby in it was floating 'round in the water drowned. They never got nary a lick of labor and nary a red penny for ary one of them babies. (Ida Blackshear Hutchinson, Arkansas)[24]

Quiet Moments

One night, Mother sat up in her bed rocking Baby while the older two boys snored soundly next to her.

"Baby" was a stretch, since her youngest child was almost two harvests old, but she still saw the infant he'd been in his toddling steps, down-soft hair, and smooth, unblemished skin. He had formed those sweet, sugary lips around a few new words: "Dada," "Mother," "Granny," and "Missus."

"Dada" only visited him twice a week, walking the long miles between his plantation and theirs on calloused feet, body bent and tired but eyes still twinkling to see his son.

"Mother" worked in the fields for most of the day, back bent in mindless labor over miles of cotton, chest heaving, thoughts caressing that sweet little boy.

"Granny" was not their biological grandmother; rather, she was a stooped old woman too old to work the fields who earned her keep watching the young'uns during the day. She did not have time to rock the children, to trace the bridge of their noses, the pucker of their lips, the buds of their closed eyes with tender fingers. She fed them grits mixed with fatback from a trough like little piglets and didn't bother diapering them. So they scuttled in her yard naked as jaybirds, supple skin easy prey for the harsh and blinding Mississippi sun.

"Missus" was the white woman who ran the plantation where Mother and Baby dwelled. She came to view the "pickaninnies," cooing at them like they were puppies in a storefront window, sweet and unkempt ruffians who need to be trained and housebroken to make the ideal pets.

House . . . broken, Mother thought, bending her nose to smell her baby's warm, sweet breath, smiling bitterly as the moments with her child coalesced into minutes and stretched over hours.

"Home" was another word her baby could say, though the cramped and weather-beaten cabin barely met its definition. Two big, gaping maws carved into the front served as windows, and an ill-fitting door let the bugs and heat in. Baby's father strung together quite a few weekends to build the bedframe where Mother now sat cross-legged over a makeshift quilt stuffed with old clothes. The room was bare but serviceable, since Mother worked from "can't see to can't see" out in the fields, only coming here to sleep.

"Broken" was not a word that Baby knew yet, but it perfectly described the state of his mother's heart. She was broken for the constant want of him, her two other boys, her little girl who had been sold, and her little girl who had died. She missed their first steps, their first words, and their first discoveries while she bent double in the field keeping Marse and Missus wealthy. She stole moments with her sons when she should have been sleeping and stumbled out into the world still tired, moving blindly in the misty half dark, her feet having long since memorized the trail from broken home to cotton fields.

She remembered what she felt when she knew with soul-deep clarity that she was carrying another child after Little Girl. All her joy suffused with the sorrow of knowing she would spend most of his formative years apart from him, knowing she would only get to hold him in snatches: in the bleary mornings or the groggy evenings; during two breaks where she rushed to breastfeed him before the overseer told her time was up; on holidays, when they only worked half a day and got to spend the other half with their families; at night, when she should be sleeping but couldn't stop looking at the beautiful child, limp, languid, and peaceful in her arms.

They were heavier every day—the baby and the burden of being apart from him.

"You're stuck here now," Cook had told her. "Can't run with no child by your side. And you ain't the type to leave him."

Mother had never been the type to run anyway. She didn't feel the bravery of other women, who had set off with their children in tow or left them in Granny's care to brave the woods with the North or the Great Dismal Swamp on their minds, the North Star guiding them toward freedom. Some of them she'd never seen again. Others she'd seen the very next day, skin punctured by the gnashing teeth of those braying hounds, backs flayed by the overseers' whips, ankles chafed with the chains they would wear for months on end until they'd learned the cost of seeking freedom.

Mother pulled Baby closer to her chest, so close she could pretend that they were wearing the same skin again. That he was safely tucked beneath her ribcage, heartbeats intertwined, fates irrevocably tied. She knew he was permanently unsafe outside of her body, that the ties that bound them could be so quickly snapped by the Missus or the overseer or the speculator who sometimes came calling, looking for fresh flesh to auction off to the highest bidder.

But then the rooster crowed.

Mother sighed.

She'd barely slept for looking down at Baby and her older boys, barely closed her eyes for fear of missing a moment breathing in the scent of his soft, warm palms, trying to inhale every detail of this beautiful little boy. She didn't do this every night. Some nights she was far too exhausted to savor him and slept with her arms tangled around him, treasuring him only in her unconscious state, her other two boys crowding her in the narrow bed.

But there was something about last night that pulled her heart to him, that told her to take in every moment.

Like her own mother did all those years before, she would pass him to Granny while he was still asleep, and Granny would pass him back at the end of the day, when he was almost sleeping once again. One of her older boys would come to the fields to pick with her, the other would stay behind to help Granny with the little children. And Mother would wonder if her baby even knew her, if he could pick her out of the scores of women hunched down in the sugarcane fields because he saw her so little during his waking hours.

He did, though. He knew the scent of her, the safety of her arms, the sweet song of her heartbeat, the cadence of her voice, and the sound of her footfalls. They etched deep, permanent lines into his memories, lines he would trace with reverent fingers for the rest of his life.

And that's something.

COLLECTIVE WITNESS: ELVIRA'S STORY

Elvira Boles was ninety-four years old when she was interviewed in El Paso, Texas, in 1937, though she wasn't quite sure of her age when asked by her interviewer. She lived with her only surviving child, Minnie Steptoe. Her other nine children had long since died.

Elvira's story started with her own childhood, which appeared to be motherless. She was the child of the master, but the wife of her enslaver did not want his illegitimate daughter underfoot. Elvira did not know how old she was when she was sold to Boles, but she did know she was old enough to be put to backbreaking labor.

"I toted brick back and put 'em down where they had to be. Six bricks each load all day. . . . I was worked to death."

She was seventeen when she married but had already borne a son to Boles because "if they had a pretty girl they would take 'em, and I's one of 'em." She remembered hating to leave that baby crying in the yard every day. "But I couldn't stay. I'd be glad to get back to my baby," she said.

Elvira described her living quarters as modest: a log cabin with a dirt floor. But rather than come back to her cabin at the end of the day and fling herself into the bed with tired abandon, Elvira stayed up at night creating beauty: "I worked late and made pretty quilts."

In 1863, after the Emancipation Proclamation, Elvira's Mississippi enslavers fled to Texas in hopes of keeping their human property. During the hurried and hard move, Elvira lost a baby: "It's buried somewhere on the road."

Elvira described freedom as difficult. "Oh, they was awful times. We just worked from place to place after freedom."[25]

Hearing how hard her life was before and after freedom, was there ever a moment, perhaps when Elvira was making quilts in her modest cabin by candlelight, her children snoring around her, when she knew true peace and belonging? Was she able to create that sense of peace and belonging for her children, a sense that had been stolen from her when she was sold away from her mother as early as six years old?

Did Elvira bask in the security of holding her children close after emancipation? Was she at rest at ninety-four, with people who loved her and cared for her as tenderly as she'd tried to care for her offspring all those years ago?

Was she glad to be back with her last baby for good?

One can only hope. Hope breathes life into the fragments of this much bigger story.

CHAPTER SIX

Lost One

My mammy would hit me in the mouth when I asked how old I was.

Ann Matthews, Tennessee

The white folks whispered about a war. Said President Abraham Lincoln wanted to free the slaves.

Cook brought her reports back from the Big House to the slave quarters at night, and the speculation flew. Some folks truly believed that freedom could be hovering at their doorstep. Others were far more suspicious since there'd already been a so-called freedom war one hundred years ago that didn't have anything to do with Negroes getting their freedom.

When Cook could pilfer discarded newspapers, she brought them for Mother to read to everyone in the hollow where they gathered to pray some evenings. Mother refused to go to their worship services—she'd seen her mother howl and pray to little effect—but she would come to read headlines that heralded a president who put slavery in jeopardy.

But she also read slave announcements in these newspapers. On September 24, 1862, the *Hinds County Gazette* reported:

> At a public sale of slaves which recently took place at Charleston, the lot, 27 in number, sold for $20,670—average, $765 each. One girl of 21 years, brought $13,230; one girl of 18 brought $1,110; one fellow of 24 brought $925; one fellow of 24, brought $1,100; one girl, 15, brought $930; one woman, 40, girl 16, girl 14, boy 12, and boy 5, sold in a family brought $4,400, average $880 each; one woman, 26, and child 18 months, brought $1500, average $750 each. Pretty fair prices considering the perils of the country, and the assurance from Washington, that the institution shall be wiped out.[1]

There were no names given for any of the twenty-seven people who had been sold together. There were no names given for any slave who was sold. Even in the slave ledgers, which kept careful account of the goings-on on the plantation, from birth to death, people were often listed simply by sex and approximate age. The same was true for Mother. Nowhere was her name written down after her purchase. Nowhere was written the name she gave her daughter who was sold away.

Five years ago, Sun had held her hand when he thought she might be dying in labor, flouting the threat of his master's ire to do so. His punishment for that crime had been more than he or his wife had imagined: when their youngest baby was two years old, Sun had been sold much too far away to visit now. If this war did pan out in their favor, would she ever find her daughter or husband? Would her mother even be able to find her?

Since then, she had explained to her sons that she called Cook "Mama" and had done so for much longer than she'd assigned the title to her birth mother. When they asked about their other grandmama, Mother didn't have much to share. She did not remember her mother's name. Sometimes she wondered if she even remembered her face.

Did it stare back at her in the occasional times she saw her own face in the looking glass? Did she have the slope of Mama's nose, the slant of her lips, the exact coil of her hair? Would the mother know the daughter if their paths crossed, seeing in her a reflection of herself? Or would they pass one another in the street without acknowledgment because they were strangers now, forever?

The thought hurt Mother's heart.

When she watched the rare families who had been reunited or, more poignantly, had never been parted, her heart ached with missing her own mother. And her grandmother? Her grandmother's mother? Those were an even more hopeless mystery beyond solving.

She was a Lost One now, trying to hold the remnants of her new little family intact.

COLLECTIVE WITNESS: THE CHANCE FOR REUNION

Samuel Simeon Andrews, "affectionally called Parson," was eighty-five years old when Rachel Austin sat down to interview him. Austin contributed five interviews to the Florida arm of the Works Progress Administration, though her daily responsibilities were more secretarial.[2] She was one of the handful of Black interviewers, which likely set Parson at ease as he told his story.

In a rather thorough interview, Austin records the story of Parson's only interaction with his grandmother:

> "Speculators" (persons who traveled from place to place with slaves for sale) had housed 84 slaves there—many of whom were pregnant women. Besides "Parson," two other slave-children, Ed Jones who now lives in Sparta, Georgia, and George Bailey were born in Tatum Square that night. The morning after their births, a woman was sent from the nearby A. J. Lane plantation to take care of the three mothers; this nurse proved to be "Parson's" grandmother. His mother told him afterwards that the meeting of mother and daughter was very jubilant, but silent and pathetic, because neither could with safety show her pleasure in finding the other. At the auction which was held a few days later, his mother, Rachel, and her two sons, Solomon Augustus and her infant who was later to be known as "Parson," were purchased by A. J. Lane,

> who had previously bought "Parson's" father, Willis, from a man named Dolphus of Albany, Georgia; thus were husband and wife reunited. (Samuel Simeon Andrews, Florida)[3]

The cyclical nature of slavery and the buying and selling of human property resulted in Parson being separated from his entire family once again before the Civil War was over. But when it ended, he was again able to find his mother and his siblings: brothers Solomon Augustus, San Francisco, Simon Peter, Lewis, Carter, and Powell Wendell, and sisters Lizzie and Ann.

These reunion stories are not far-fetched. Several interviewees remember being found by their mothers after enslavement. But to a child, they were found so soon after slavery because their parents knew exactly where to look.

When children were taken states away, the odds of their parents being able to locate them after the Civil War dwindled. Last names were sometimes changed to match their enslavers. Sometimes they would occasionally leave the places where they'd originally enslaved their human chattel for various reasons. Sometimes enslavers sold their human property repeatedly.

After the war, ads for finding lost loved ones littered newspapers. People would cite everything they knew about the places where their kindred had last been owned. The *Southwestern Christian Advocate* came to have a running column called "Lost Friends," which was often read in church with the hope that someone who had a connection to the lost loved one would be able to make reunion a reality.[4]

> Dear Editor—I want to hear from my son, Lewis Hickerson. When last heard from he was at Como, Panola Co., Miss. His father's name is Harrison Thompson. He left Manchester, Coffee county, Tenn., in 1863. A daughter, Victory, was sold from the same place in 1865, to Dr. Singleton. When last heard from she was at Fairfield, Bedford Co., Tenn. Address your mother at Hillsboro, Coffee Co., Tenn, care of Rev. J. Summerhill. (Jennie Rutlege)

Mr. Editor—I wish to inquire for my wife and children. Wife's name was Nancy. She used to belong to Madison Gunn, in Chicka Co., Miss., and he sold her to R. D. Dick Price in 1862, and he sold her and children on Flint Creek, in Ga. I had by my wife five children, John, Reuben, and Matt. I ask all the preachers to read this in their churches, and if they are found, write me at Moss Point, Jackson Co., Miss., in care of Rev. N. Cannon. (Lewis Wright)

Mr. Editor—I desire some information about my mother. The last time I saw her I was in Alexandria, Virginia, about the year 1852 or 1853. Her name was Hannah. She belonged to Lawyer Gibbs who sold her when I was quite young to a trader named Bruthing. Later, Gibbs lived at Leesburg, Va., where he sold mother to Bruthing, and afterwards Tibbs moved to Alexandria, Va., and swapped me to Bruthing for another boy. Bruthing put me in jail and I cried, so he told me if I would hush he would bring my mother the next morning; which he did; but I was so young mother hardly knew me, and Bruthing stood four or five boys in a line and asked her which one of them was her boy. She stood a few moments and then said I was the boy. Mother then brought me some cake and candy, and that was the last time I saw her. (Henry Gibbs)[5]

Sometimes successful reunions resulted from these advertisements. Other times they didn't. But the formerly enslaved were dogged in their quest to reunite with their family members.

Robert Glenn of North Carolina was sold away from his family when he was just a boy. The twists and turns of his story finally brought him back home to North Carolina to surprise his mother "if she was still living." By now, he was a grown man who'd gone to Illinois to seek his fortune and perhaps better treatment in a northern state than what he'd encountered in the South of his youth.

Robert tried to surprise his mother, asking his companions to call him by a different name when he knocked on her door. But she knew him:

> "Ain't you my child? Tell me ain't you my child whom I left on the road near Mr. Moore's before the war?" I broke down and began to cry. Mother nor father did not know me, but mother suspicioned I was her child. Father had a few days previously remarked that he did not want to die without seeing his son once more. I could not find language to express my feeling. I did not know before I came home whether my parents were dead or alive. This Christmas I spent in the county and state of my birth and childhood, with mother, father, and freedom, was the happiest period of my entire life because those who were torn apart in bondage and sorrow several years previous were now united in freedom and happiness. (Robert Glenn, North Carolina)[6]

Such a reunion did not await everyone who set out to find their loved ones. So many stories end like Bethany and Jerry Veney's story, parting never to be seen again in this life:

> They sold my sister Lucy and my brother Fred in slavery time, and I have never seen 'em in my life. Mother would cry when she was telling me about it. She never seen 'em anymore. I just couldn't bear to hear her tell it without crying. They were carried to Richmond, and sold by old master when they were children. (Lizzie Baker, North Carolina)[7]

> At times pathetic scenes prevailed in the selling of slaves; namely, the separation of mother and child. Often, a boy or girl would be sold and taken away from his or her mother. In many cases the parting would be permanent and the child and its mother would never see each other again. (Tinie Force and Elvira Lewis, Kentucky)[8]

> Angeline was his oldest sister and Emmaline was his twin sister. He never seen any of his people again. He forgot their names. (Jennie Davis, Arkansas)[9]

> My oldest brother was sold to Virginia and shipped down into Texas about ten years before I was born and I ain't never seen him. (Norman Burkes, Arkansas)[10]

Some were still looking for their loved ones even when interviewed in 1937, seventy years after emancipation:

> Ellaine said she would never forget the few words her mother spoke to her just before they were separated. “Ellaine, honey mamma’s going way off and ain’t never going to see her baby again.” An I can see myself holdin’ onto my mamma and both of us crying—and then, she was gone and I never seed her since. I hopes I goin’ to see my good mamma some day, I do. Yes’ I’se goin to do it son, I sure is, yes indeed. (Ellaine Wright, Missouri)[11]

MEETING MANY YEARS LATER

One of the rarer side effects of the combination of broken family ties and an enterprise that relied almost exclusively on a Black woman’s ability to bear her enslaver many children was the threat of incest. These stories litter slave accounts as horror stories and cautionary tales passed from place to place rather than first-person experiences of the interviewees.

I have heard my grandmother talk about slaves being put on the block and sold and then meeting way years after and not knowing one another. She told me about a woman who was separated from her son. One day, years after slavery, when she had married again and had a family, she and her husband got to talking about old slave times. She told him about how she had been sold away from her baby son when he was a little thing. She told him how he had a certain scar on his arm. Her husband had a similar scar and he got to talking about slave times, and they found out that they were mother and son. He left her and went on his way sad because he didn’t want to stay on living as husband with his mother. I don’t think those people were held accountable for that, do you? (Cora L. Horton, Arkansas)[12]

A man once married his ma and didn't know it. He was sold from her when about eight years old. When he grow to a young men, slavery then was over, he met this woman who he liked and so they were married. They was married a month when one night they started to tell of their experiences and how many times they was sold. The husband told how he was sold from his mother who liked him dearly. He told how his ma fainted when they took him away and how his master then used to brand his baby slaves at a year old. When he showed her the brand she fainted 'cause she then realized that she had married her son. (Augustus Ladson, South Carolina)[13]

This is essentially a true story. An old ex-slave told it to me. . . .

"You know, Pierre, this scar on the back of your head sets me a-thinkin' way back when I was a gal on old Master Haynes's plantation at Lafourche. I had a little brother then. He was 'bout two years younger than me. I was just 'bout eight years old myself." Tears streamed down Tamerant's cheeks. She checked a sob, sighed, and continued her story. "Well, the master sold my little brother from us, and five years later they sold me from my ma and pa. Since then I ain't seen none of my folks. But this is what I wants to tell you 'bout the scar. One day my little brother and me was playin', and he hit me and hurt me. I took a oyster shell and cut him on the back of his head right where you got that scar on your head."

Pierre jumped up from the chair before Tamerant finished her story. His eyes bulged almost out of their sockets; his lips swung open; his face streamed with perspiration. He stood stupefied, as a man entranced with nightmare.

"What's the matter with you Pierre, honey? You looks like you seen a ha'nt."

Pierre droned in a voice pregnant with despair.

"I is that little brother you cut in de head, Tamerant!"[14]

Rebuilding a Legacy

Lost One didn't have a story to pass down to her children.

She didn't know where her mother had come from or who her people were. She didn't know how long they'd been in the United States or what country they'd come from on the vast continent of Africa that the older slaves sometimes spoke about.

"CILLER WAS THE DAUGHTER OF A KING IN AFRICA"

Marse Starke was a rich man. He had in the Quarter what was know'd as a children's house. A nurse stayed in it all the time to care for all the plantation children. My granny "Kissy" acted as nurse there some. Aunt Peggy and aunt Ciller was two more. Ciller was the daughter of a King in Africa, but that story been traveling ever since she got to these shores, and it still a-going. (Unnamed Informant, South Carolina)[15]

Our great-grandmother was named granny Flora. They stole her from Africa with a red pocket handkerchief. Old man John William got my great-grandmother. The people in New England got scared of we n——. They were afraid we would rise against 'em and they pushed us on down South. Lawd, why didn't they let us stay where we was, they never wouldn't a been so many half white n——, but the old master was to blame for that. (Hannah Crasson, North Carolina)[16]

Grandfather was a South Carolinian. Master Harris bought him, two more, his brothers and two sisters and his mother at one time. He was real African. Grandma on mother's side was dark Indian. She had white hair nearly straight. I have some of it now. Mother was lighter. That is where I gets my light color. (Mary Gaines, Arkansas)[17]

She didn't even know her mother's first name.

She didn't know the last name of her first enslaver.

All she knew was her mother's face, and even that felt like it was fading after so many years away.

When she was a girl in the Big House, she had sat in on Little Missy's lessons about American history. Missy could trace her ancestry all the way back to the *Mayflower*, she'd told her tutor, preening. Probably even Jamestown, she'd said. They were some of the first people to come to Mississippi and drive out the native folks who had been living there before. She recited the name of this or that grandfather and talked about places across the sea they'd come from: Scotland, England, and Germany. Missy had a last name, even a name right there in the middle. She knew her exact birthday, August 9, and she knew her mama's birthday too.

Lost One knew the seasons of her children's births by the work she had been doing and the weather outside when she went into labor. She kept track of those seasons with tally marks every time the wind changed so that she had an approximation of her boys' ages—and her girl's, wherever she was. But she had no tally marks for her own age, and certainly not for her mother's.

When her oldest boy's questions about her past could not be sated even by Lost One putting her foot down, she relented. She told him what she knew, and then told him what she didn't know and why.

She told him that, once upon a time, his grandfather or great-grandfather had been born in a faraway place called Africa. She didn't talk about Africa the way some folks did, going on and on about its darkness and unholiness. Instead, she told him about the Africa she imagined, a place even older than this one with bigger trees and deeper rivers and clearer streams. She told him that she'd heard there were kings there, and queens, and slaves too, probably. That they had their own wars, their own ways, and their own beauty.

She told her son about the boat that had brought this ancestor from their homeland, carrying them on choppy waters to a brand-new country. She reasoned that since Sun had lived ten miles from them before and now lived several days' journey from them even though he was still in the same state, the trip across the water from Africa must have taken weeks—maybe even months.

When she was unsure, she borrowed details from other stories that she'd heard, stories from elders about their own experiences crossing the water. She did not spare the young boy any detail he asked. She told him that people were packed together on top of each other, that it was dank, dark, and dirty in the ship's hold, and that the roiling water sometimes made them lose control of their stomachs and their bowels. She told him that some folks chose to jump into the sea rather than be ferried to an unknown land, and that some people tried to overcome their captors and at times it worked.

Cook scolded her for putting such ideas into the mind of her young son. "Children shouldn't have to think on such things!"

But her son had to think on the whippings he witnessed. He had to think on knowing that his father had been taken away from him, and that he'd likely never see or hear from him again. He had to think on understanding that someone else decided whether they would stay together as a family or be cast to the wind like chaff, blown God knows where, never to be gathered again.

So when her son asked, Lost One answered. She told him about slave auctions, about how she remembered standing on the block after the speculator first bought her and having Marse bid more for her when he found out how many siblings she had. And she told him that she didn't know any of her siblings' names since she had been so young when she was ripped away from them.

There was something healing in the telling. Lost One finally started to understand that *she* was her son's history now—*she* was his legacy. His story began with her. And if she was able to hold on to him, perhaps she would be the beginning of his children's stories, and their children's stories, and their children's stories after them.

As she told each story, she quilted, just like her mother, sitting up by candlelight and weaving scraps of cloth into something beautiful. And as she healed her heart through storytelling, she realized she was finally ready to incorporate that little scrap of old cloth into this new work she was making. She was finally able to make a quilt with little pieces from everyone she loved—her Mama included. She didn't have to hold the scrap to remember Mama. Those memories weren't going anywhere.

There were other people who knew more about where they came from. Cook talked about a place in Africa called "Congo" and her own father's arrival to America, though never in front of her grandchildren. And that, Lost One realized, was *also* her children's story, even if it wasn't hers. Sun was half of their legacy too, and they knew Cook, and they knew Congo now.

She sewed the story of her sons together for them like a quilt, piecemeal, filching and hoarding like a magpie. She kept the ugly parts in but focused on the beautiful ones.

"I don't remember my mother's name," she said, "but I remember a song she used to sing":

> No more auction block for me
> No more, no more
> No more auction block for me
> Many thousands gone
> Many thousands gone

Thousands of people and their stories. Stories that should have belonged to Lost One. Stories that should have belonged to her sons.

She told them about Auntie too, even though she was pretty sure Auntie hadn't actually been her mother's sister. Because she knew that family could also be chosen. Cook had chosen her long before she'd married Sun.

> Sometimes I feel like a motherless child,
> Sometimes I feel like a motherless child,
> Sometimes I feel like a motherless child,
> A long way from home, a long way from home.

Sometimes I feel like I'm almost done,
Sometimes I feel like I'm almost done,
Sometimes I feel like I'm almost done,
And a long, long way from home, a long way from home.

"But you're not motherless," her son told her once when she related this memory.

And she smiled. Because he was right. As far as she knew, her mother was still out there, about Cook's age, alive and well, and maybe the mother of more children after her. Maybe her mother's heart ached for Lost One just as Lost One's ached for her own lost daughter. But maybe, too, just like Lost One, she had learned to survive with a gaping wound at the very center of her because she had to.

"Not fatherless either," Cook said, even though Lost One had even less notion about her father than she did about her mother.

Lost One scoffed a bit. Cook was always trying to get her to go to worship services down in the hollow. Though she'd let Cook take the boys, she almost never went along. She remembered her mother's prayers and how God hadn't answered them. She remembered how much Mama had loved God, but she also remembered that God had forsaken them.

She gathered her children to her chest. Reframing her history as the collection of stories she passed on to them made her feel less lost. Holding them close and trusting that she would be able to watch them grow up, and to watch them pass these stories on to their children, made her feel more whole.

She could start their legacy anew.

COLLECTIVE WITNESS: **JANE'S STORY**

In 1858, a slaveholder named Thomas Nelson wrote a deed bequeathing a Black woman named Jane, along with her four children —Sanders, Laura, Minerva, and Eveline—to his daughter Ann.

As was customary in a deed of this sort, he bequeathed Jane, her children, and their children in perpetuity. Thomas owned at least ten slaves in 1858, and it's unclear why he was bequeathing Jane and her four children (half of his property) to his daughter so far in advance of his 1871 death—or why Ann had been chosen over her three brothers, two of whom were older, and her sister.

What *has* become clear, due to the ancestry research of Thomas Nelson's descendants, is that he was likely the father of Jane's four children: Sanders, Laura, Minerva, and Eveline. Ann was the half sister of Jane's children—the children who became her slaves.

Thomas's line of ancestry goes back to William Dandridge of Norfolk in Worcester, England, and Euphan Wallace of Goochland, Virginia. The couple married August 17, 1715, in Hampton, Virginia, when they were both eighteen years old. The Dandridges even make an appearance in a seven-volume history series published in the early twentieth century called *Colonial Families of the United States of America: In Which Is Given the History, Genealogy and Armorial Bearings of Colonial Families Who Settled in the American Colonies from the Time of the Settlement of Jamestown, 13th May, 1607, to the Battle of Lexington, 19th April, 1775*.

Jane's line of known ancestry begins with her.

Her mother is listed as a "Chattel Slave Unknown." Her father's name is also unknown. Little is known about Jane's life after the sale, but she lived in Alcorn County, Mississippi, and died there in 1917.

Her youngest daughter, Eveline, married a formerly enslaved man named William Younger. William's known ancestry extends back a bit further than Eveline's—to an Alexander Younger, born in 1800. The couple had several children together, and their daughter Essie married David McCline and had a daughter whom she named for her mother: Eva Lena.

Eva Lena had a daughter named Merlene in 1919.

Merlene had a son in 1940.

That son had a daughter in 1966.

And that daughter had a daughter in 1990.

This last daughter, born in 1990, would take the time to try to unravel the long and winding history of every part of her family tree—her paternal grandfather and grandmother, her maternal grandfather and grandmother, her spouse's maternal and paternal grandparents. She would run into a host of roadblocks, like the fact that, between them, she and her spouse only had one living grandparent (and that grandparent was the youngest of the four of them) and no living great-grandparents. She would run into roadblocks again and again as the trail of one family history ran cold, only to pick up again with the white ancestry of the slaveholders who were also part of her family line.

She would run across so many stories. A fourteen-year-old who gave birth to her enslaver's child. A young family who moved to Los Angeles during the Great Migration. Deep Texas roots that wound their way back to her chosen home of Mississippi. She would find Confederate soldiers—assuredly enough to qualify her to become a member of the United Daughters of the Confederacy. (She'd pass.) She would find men who fought in the Revolutionary War—and all of the war heroes would be the white slaveholding fruit of her family tree.

But the story she would return to again and again would be the story of Jane Nelson.

She is me.

When Thomas Nelson had that deed written, he gave Ann not just Jane, Sanders, Laura, Minerva, and Eveline but also their "heirs and their issue." He gave her Jane, Eveline, Essie, Eva Lena, Merlene—and, though her name isn't written in the deed, he gave her the daughter who was born in 1966 and the daughter who was born in 1990 too.

It just so happened that this deed was written half a decade before the Emancipation Proclamation was issued. But if it had been written one hundred years sooner—in 1758 instead of 1858—all of those generations would have been born in chains except for the last two, simply because of *Partus Sequitur Ventrem*—simply because their branch of the tree diverted with Jane and not with her half sister and eventual enslaver, Tabitha.

If the deed had been written in 1758, my mother would have been the very first member of the family tree not born into slavery.

If the deed had been written in 1658, we still wouldn't have gotten to the part of the family tree that was born free.

There are a lot of *ifs* here, and, ultimately, the hypothetical is just that—a hypothetical. The deed was written in 1858. The Civil War ended in 1865. What-ifs have their limitations.

But there *were* deeds that were written in 1758. There *were* deeds that were written in 1658. There *were* people who were born into slavery for hundreds of years, and whose family lines were lost to the enterprise. And there are people who look back across the vast history of chattel slavery and find it impossible to eke out a story of their own.

Their story has been lost, just as Lost One's was.

And perhaps, someday, they will dig deep enough to find the piece of information that unlocks the beauty and sorrow of their family tree.

But as is the case with so many of the people who searched for loved ones and lost friends in the wake of the Civil War—perhaps not.

INTERLUDE

Elizabeth[1]

Elizabeth's immediate desire was to protect them—to shield them—the two young Black men who showed up at her front door.

She stepped into the room and was, perhaps, surprised to behold the two Black interviewers, Claude Anderson and his companion. They looked at her like two scientists with magnifying glasses and notebooks, keen to make their observations. They were young, gifted, and Black—educated enough for this fancy government job that had brought them to her.

They accepted her offer of a seat, and then asked her to unfold herself for them—to spread out the quilt of her personal story and act as tour guide for her trauma. The hodgepodge squares—once colorful and vibrant—were now faded. But still warm enough, threadbare though they were, to offer protection to these young Black men.

Because they were still Black. Still at the mercy of a Jim Crow South but educated enough for President Roosevelt to assign them the auspicious task of collecting stories for the Works Progress Administration.

And so they'd come here, today, ready to listen—ready to learn.

"Come on in, boys," she'd said, sounding downright jolly. "Sure am glad to see ya. You're lookin' so well. That's what I say. Fight boys! You're doing all right."

Proud.

She was full to bursting with pride at the young men who sat across from her that day. She, who had been born a slave, had lived to see them standing there—polished professionals. She bade them to fight even as their mere existence was a battle. She bade them to fight and then encouraged them, because, from the looks of things, they were winning the battle.

Elizabeth was poor and old, weathered and lonely, but they looked spit-shined and polished, ready to ask her about hardship they'd never had to endure for themselves. Thank God for that.

They chose that moment to remind her of the reason for their meeting. Elizabeth waved them away.

"What's that?" she demurred. "You want me to tell you 'bout slavery days? Well, I kin tell ya, but I ain't. S'all past now, so I say let 'er rest. It's too awful to tell anyway."

She wanted them to be warmed by her presence but not to look too closely at what constituted that presence—at the survival that had brought her to this place. She wanted to warm them with the years of love she'd stored up for the next generation—the years of hope she'd carried for them. But she didn't want them to get too close to that hope's need lest it burn them.

Elizabeth was dazzled by how pristine they appeared, talking to this woman who had witnessed and fought through an unfair share of suffering. She wanted to protect them from the past—to shield them so they could live a life unencumbered by her pain.

"I'm fine. Don't worry about me. Just keep going. Keep fighting. I'll be all right."

When they pressed, undeterred by her praise and encouragement, she finally told them a bit in fits and starts. The story gushed out in some places, trickled out in others—and at some points, stopped entirely.

She didn't mean to speak so freely, but once she started unearthing the words she'd kept inside for so long, it became difficult to hold them back. She spoke of a mistress who was a good woman.

"'Course, I mean she'd slap an' beat you once in a while," she said.

But she said less about others.

"Tain't no sense for you to know about all those mean white folks," Elizabeth said, catching herself before she started going into detail about too much abuse.

But Claude and his companion had a job to do—the same job that had them suited and booted and Elizabeth spilling over with pride. So they pressed Ms. Sparks, coaxing out story after story:

> She was nineteen when she married John in 1861, and had her first son in 1862. The little boy was three years old when the Emancipation Proclamation freed their little family. They were thrust out into a brand-new free world, looking forward with hope and anticipation that Jim Crow would soon dash. When she was first set free, she thought she might have a son like these boys—successful, well-kept, and polished. Instead, the manual labor that had dogged her in slavery had been their lot. The work was honorable, and they came by their money honestly. But Elizabeth had never gotten to see her children rest.

She told them more. Her mother worked in the big house doing laundry. She had five sisters and five brothers.

But then, they hit another wall.

"Might as well quit lookin' at me. I ain't gonna tell you any more," she said, stony.

There was so much Elizabeth didn't want them to know—so much she didn't want them to carry. Then, too, there was her own fear.

"Can't tell yer all I know. Ole Shep might come back and get me. Why if I was to tell you the really bad things, some of them dead white folks would come right up out of their graves. Well, I'll tell some more, but I can't tell all."

She feared her old master even from beyond the grave. Even several decades removed from his influence over her life. Her Pavlovian response at the mention of his name was to hide her true feelings for her own safety.

Again and again, she uttered the familiar refrain, "Can't tell all." But as their meeting was winding down, she added, "God's got all."

And besides, she told them, "The end a time is at hand anyway." Jesus was coming back on the clouds any day. Elizabeth's hopes were tied up in the hereafter—in the yonder—and in the future that these two young Black men represented with their success.

They finished their meeting the same way they started it, the ninety-five-year-old woman cracking a smile and saying, "Goodbye. Keep looking good and come again."

CHAPTER SEVEN

Sister

We had to steal away at night to have church on the ditch bank, and crawl home on the belly. Once overseer heard us praying, give us one day each 100 lashes.

Elvira Boles, Texas

Honey, is you a Christian? I hopes you is, 'cause you is too fine looking for to go to hell.

Katherine Eppes, Alabama

Trustin' was the only hope of the poor black critters in them days. Us jest prayed for strength to endure it to the end. We didn't 'spect nothin' but to stay in bondage till we died.

Delia Garlic, Alabama

Cook's funeral is what finally did it.

Lost One knew that her mother-in-law would have wanted her to attend the service in the grove, and she wanted to honor her this one last time. So she made her way to the hollow late that night, alongside most of the other slaves from the quarters.

They'd already had a funeral of sorts. Marse had the preacher come and say a few words when they lowered Cook into the ground. But the preacher mostly talked about how Cook had been a "faithful servant" to her "master and mistress," and how everyone would do well to abide by her example. The white minister said she had her reward in heaven now for being such a well-behaved darkie. To hear him speak, Cook had gone up yonder just to be some other white person's slave in heaven.

"NOTHING ABOUT JESUS WAS EVER SAID"

We went to church not the play and you ought to hear that preaching. Obey your mass and missy, don't steal chicken and eggs and meat, but nary a word about having a soul to save. (Jacob Branch, Texas)[1]

Nothing about Jesus was ever said and the overseers stood there to see the preacher talked as he wanted him to talk. (Charlie Van Dyke, Alabama)[2]

Before freedom we always went to white churches on Sundays with passes but they never mentioned God; they just always told us to be "good n——" and mind our missus and masters. (Clayborn Gantling, Florida)[3]

Lost One knew that the service in the hollow would be different. They waited until everyone in the Big House was good and asleep before they set out. As always, someone stayed behind as a lookout. Normally, Lost One was the one who volunteered to make the whippoorwill trill that would alert the watchman on the edge of the woods to run down and warn the others to disperse. They always tried to keep things quiet, but even when they caught the Spirit and got a little louder than they ought, the distance between the hollow and the Big House was enough to keep them safe under cover of night.

As much as Marse and Missus talked about religion, their slaves were not allowed to fellowship together. The house slaves were permitted to sit in segregated church services every Sunday, but those who lived in the quarters had to content themselves with Christmas and funeral sermons when the old white preacher decided to come out and bless them with his presence.

"THE SLAVES HAD SECRET PRAYER MEETINGS"

There was no church on the plantation and we were not allowed to have prayer meetings. (Louisa Adams, North Carolina)[4]

The slaves had secret prayer meetings with pots turned down to kill the sound of the singing. We sang a song, "I'm glad to salvation's free." Once they heard us, next morning they took us and tore our backs to pieces. They would say, "Are you free? What were you singin' about freedom?" (Charity Austin, North Carolina)[5]

The white folks wouldn't let the slaves pray, if they got to pray it was while walking behind the plow. White folks would whip the slaves if they heard them sing or pray. (Millie Simpkins, Tennessee)[6]

Some believed they'd git freedom and others didn't. They had places they met and prayed for freedom. They stole out in some of their houses and turned a washpot down at the door. (Laura Abromson, Arkansas)[7]

Lost One had been to these services before. She watched the shuffling feet and moans of the ring shouts, felt the thrum of their humming and hymn singing deep inside of her. But she knew she was moved by their community and commonality more than by anything spiritual. Her mother had prayed to a God who clearly wasn't listening, and Lost One assumed the same thing was happening out here.

The old man who led most of the sermons got up and started talking about Cook. About how faithful she was. How kind. How she'd give you the shirt right off her back or pilfer food from the kitchen for you if you were hungry. About how she'd teach the ropes to anyone new and take others under her wing. About how she loved her children, Lost One included. And about how Lost One wasn't lost at all, but Sister to most of Cook's brood and wife to Sun.

Cook loved just like Jesus did, the old man said. She hated their chains just like Jesus did. She longed to see all the captives set free, just like Jesus did.

If Jesus wanted that, and his Father God was all-powerful, then why didn't he just bring it to pass? Sister wondered.

The old man looked at her as though she'd said the words aloud. "This is an evil world," he said, mournfully. "It was never meant to be such, but sin entered and marred everything. Turned brother against brother, as far back as Cain and Abel, son against father, as far back as Ham and Noah. God wiped out that evil, once upon a time, with the great flood. But afterward, he put his bow in the heavens to remind us that he wouldn't handle evil that way again. He wouldn't flood the whole world—he'd send his only Son to the world to die for it."

Sister had her arms around her children. She shifted uncomfortably from foot to foot. She'd heard this message many times before because Cook couldn't help but proselytize her. But somehow, this time felt different.

"He takes smaller steps toward wiping out the evil now," the old man said. "And those steps feel mighty long, don't they?"

"Yes," Sister answered, but she wasn't the only one speaking. All around her, a world-weary cacophony of "Yes," and "Mm hm," and "Say that, Pastor" was building.

"He's waiting," the old man said. "He's waiting for all of his lost ones to come home. Every last one. Some of the ones who are committing the evil right now, he's waiting for them to see the light and run to him. And you might say, 'Preacher! I want him to stop waiting!' But, my child, if he had stopped waiting a moment sooner, he wouldn't have been able to welcome some of you."

Sister felt the prick of tears behind her eyes. She shook her head and cleared her throat, trying to move past the lump she felt there. She was trembling, even as the sticky summer heat enveloped her.

"The mystery of the Trinity is that he sent his Son," said the preacher. "But God and his Son and his Spirit are one and the same. He gave himself. What more could the God of the universe give than himself? Do you want to know what giving your whole self looks like?" he asked. "It looks like Cook's life."

This time, one of the amens came from Sister's lips. Because what could be truer? If there was a God, and if his Son, Jesus, had walked sacrificially in this world, then Cook had been one of his best disciples.

"If you want to see how God is stopping the evil in this world, look at Cook," the preacher said. "Look at the love she had for each and every one of you. Look at the light she brought into this dark place. That light? That's what the gospel is all about. My, how it shines."

COLLECTIVE WITNESS: A PERSECUTED CHURCH

The religion of the enslaved was often encouraged only so far as it benefited the enslaver, just like their marriages, the bearing of their children, and every single other aspect of enslaved life. If that benefit was not clear, then the practices were not allowed.

Some enslavers made sure to expose their enslaved to religion. They brought them to church and made them sit in on segregated services, where part of the sermon might even be addressed toward them:

No prayer meetings allowed on the plantation but we went to Salem to white folks church. (Chaney Hews, North Carolina)[8]

We sat in the back of the church just like we sits in the back of the streetcars nowadays. (Ellen Claiborne, Georgia)[9]

Sometimes enslavers even catechized the enslaved:

The white folks, old missus, teach us the catechism, but they didn't want you to learn to read and write. (Robert Hinton, North Carolina)[10]

He always say, "Book learning don't raise no good sugar cane." The only learning he allowed was when they learn the colored children the Methodist catechism. (Ellen Betts, Texas)[11]

We'd go up to the white folks house every Sunday evening and old mistress would learn us our catechism. We'd have to comb our heads and clean up and go up every Sunday evening. She'd line us up and learn us our catechism. (Marthala Grant, Arkansas)[12]

Sometimes the enslaved were allowed to meet on their own:

Oh, yes ma'am, I used to go to meeting. Us n—— didn't have no meeting house on the plantation but Marse Jim allowed us to build a brush arbor. (Anthony Abercrombie, Alabama)[13]

We were allowed to have prayer meetings in our homes and we also went to the white folks' church. (Mary Anderson, North Carolina)[14]

On our Master's place, slaves didn't go off to meeting at all. They just went round to one another's houses and sang songs. Some of them read the Bible by heart. (Rachel Adams, Georgia)[15]

The slaves had a regular church house, which was a small size building constructed of boards. Preaching was conducted by a colored minister especially assigned to this duty. (Mack Mullen, Florida)[16]

But more often, the testimonies read like these:

> We did not have prayer meeting at master's plantation or anywhere. Master would not allow that. (Jane Arrington, North Carolina)[17]

> My father would have church in dwelling houses and they had to whisper. (Lucretia Alexander, Arkansas)[18]

Religion was not necessarily beat into them. Rather, the threat was often that religion would be beat out of them if they believed and persisted in their prayers for freedom.

Seventy-five-year-old Celestia Avery of Florida recalled the story of her grandmother, Sylvia, who refused to give up her morning prayers:

> Every morning my grandmother would pray, and old man Heard despised to hear anyone pray, saying they were only doing so that they might become free.

But Sylvia was undaunted, even in the face of the whipping she got every day "just as sure as the sun would rise." On the day of one particularly brutal beating, pregnant Sylvia was left to fend for herself in the woods. She stayed tied to a sapling all day until finally, at night, her young husband was able to sneak out and cut her down. Rather than return to the slave quarters to risk being caught praying the next morning, Sylvia went farther into the woods. She stayed there for two weeks.

When the master—described as "mean" and "not liked by any of his slaves"—found Sylvia, she had given birth to twins. Blessedly, in addition to being a praying woman, Sylvia was an experienced midwife and had wrapped both babies in pieces of her petticoats.

Interestingly enough, Sylvia's enslaver did provide a religious outlet for those he enslaved:

> Slaves were given separate churches, but the minister, who conducted the services, was white. Very seldom did the text vary from

> the usual one of obedience to the master and mistress, and the necessity for good behavior. Every one was required to attend church, however, the only self expression they could indulge in without conflict with the master was that of singing. Any one heard praying was given a good whipping; for most masters thought their prayers no good since freedom was the uppermost thought in everyone's head. (Celestia Avery, Florida)[19]

Sylvia had no way of knowing that, long after her life had ended at age 115, people would speak of her religious fervor as an act of submission rather than an act of resistance. They would say she worshiped a white man's God because the white man kept her from any spiritual knowledge of her own, that her religion had been beat into her.

She had no way of knowing that her resistance would seem to some who knew her in posterity as an act of compliance to the religion of her enslavers.

She knew better than most that this could not have been further from the truth.

"PRAY FOR THE NORTH TO WIN"

I learned to pray when very young and kept it up even in my unsaved days. My white master's folks knew me to be a praying boy, and asked me—in 1865—when the South was about whipped and General Wilson was headed our way—to pray to God to hold the Yankees back. Of course, I didn't have any love for any Yankees—and haven't now, for that matter—but I told my white folks straight-from-the-shoulder that I could not pray along those lines. I told them flat-footedly that, while I loved them and would do any reasonable praying for them, I could not pray against my conscience: that I not only wanted to be free, but that I wanted to see all the Negroes freed! (W. B. Allen, Georgia)[20]

Just before the war, a white preacher he come to us slaves and say: "Do you want to keep your homes where you get all to eat and raise your children, or do you want to be free to roam round without a home, like the wild animals? If you want to keep your homes you better pray for the South to win. All that wants to pray for the South to win, raise the hand." We raised our hand, 'cause we was scared not to, but we sure didn't want the South to win.

That night, all the slaves had a meeting down in the hollow. Old Uncle Mack, he gets up and says: "One time over in Virginia there was two old n——, Uncle Bob and Uncle Tom. They was mad at one another and one day they decided to have a dinner and bury the hatchet. So they sat down, and when Uncle Bob wasn't looking, Uncle Tom put some poison in Uncle Bob's food, but he saw it, and when Uncle Tom wasn't looking, Uncle Bob he turned the tray 'round on Uncle Tom, and he gets the poison food." Uncle Mack, he says: "That's what we slaves is going to do, just turn the tray around and pray for the North to win." (William M. Adams, Texas)[21]

A God for the Oppressed

With Cook gone, Missus needed help in the house again, and she turned to Sister. With Sister's hair shorn and her body spent from bearing five children in as many years, Missus was no longer afraid she would attract Marse's wandering eye. She was still as fragile as ever, with a wrist Sister could clasp her thumb and pointer finger around with ease.

Missy was back at home with her own child, having married a wealthy man from the coast the previous year. He was fighting in the War for Southern Independence and had taken some poor slave mother's son along with him to carry his bags and ammunition. Missy liked to say he'd had enough money to hire someone to take his place on the front, but he was so endeared to his beloved Southland that he wouldn't hear of letting someone else do his part.

After so many years of working in the fields and slave quarters, Sister found it more difficult than ever to be in the Big House. Missus was just as shrill and punishing when she was about, and Missy reverted to the needy child she'd been when Sister first played the part of her nurse so long ago. In addition to her cooking responsibilities, she was helping their house girls empty slop jars, tend fires, and dust mantels.

Sister didn't mind one part of her job: disposing of the newspapers. Though it would've been foolish of her to get caught reading twice in one lifetime and expect that lifetime to linger, she took her chances by filching pieces of information when no one was looking. Missus was too caught up in running into town to gossip about the war and those "darned Yankees" to be overseeing all the activities in the house. Marse was forever locked away in his study counting his Confederate bills. And Missy had a young baby whom she doted upon every waking hour.

Sister took the news of the headlines back to their meetings at the hollow whenever she dared, and they were grateful for the news. The enslaved on other plantations weren't always so lucky.

"God has seen fit to bring an end to our suffering," the pastor said, beaming. "He has heard our cry."

Sister scoffed. As much as she was trying not to mock Cook's Christianity anymore, she couldn't let that one slide.

"Marse says the Lord will fight the Confederates' battles," she said. "That he meant for the races to be separate ever since the curse of Ham."

"I know you look in those books sometimes, Sister," said the preacher, a twinkle in his eye. "Next time you get ahold of that family Bible, I want you to spend some time in the Psalms. Psalm 44 and 72. And Isaiah 9."

Sister threw him a quizzical look.

"No, I can't read, Sister," he said, chuckling. "It's all in here." He pointed to his head. "And in here." He pointed to his heart.

As skeptical as she was, Sister *did* find time to read the passages the preacher had mentioned to her when she was alone in the Big House. And when she did, she saw a pattern she had not expected:

> Awake, why sleepest thou, O Lord? arise, cast us not off for ever.
> Wherefore hidest thou thy face, and forgettest our affliction and our oppression?
> For our soul is bowed down to the dust: our belly cleaveth unto the earth.
> Arise for our help, and redeem us for thy mercies' sake. (Ps. 44:23–26)

> For he shall deliver the needy when he crieth; the poor also, and him that hath no helper.
> He shall spare the poor and needy, and shall save the souls of the needy.
> He shall redeem their soul from deceit and violence: and precious shall their blood be in his sight. (Ps. 72:12–14)

> The people that walked in darkness have seen a great light: they that dwell in the land of the shadow of death, upon them hath the light shined.
>
> Thou hast multiplied the nation, and not increased the joy: they joy before thee according to the joy in harvest, and as men rejoice when they divide the spoil.
>
> For thou hast broken the yoke of his burden, and the staff of his shoulder, the rod of his oppressor, as in the day of Midian. (Isa. 9:2–4)

When Sister returned to the hollow, she told the preacher about what she'd read. He beamed as she recounted Psalm 44, where the psalmist had cried out to the Lord, fearing that God had forgotten his affliction. She told him about the promise of Psalm 72, where the Lord committed to delivering the needy when they called. She told him about Isaiah 9 and a God who cared about the oppression of his people.

"Does Marse know those verses are in there?" she asked, and the preacher laughed so hard that he slapped his knee and wiped a tear from his eye.

"Why do you think he doesn't want you to read it?" he asked her.

"WHITE FOLKS DID NOT ALLOW US TO HAVE NOTHING TO DO WITH BOOKS"

No! No! Oh! No! You had better not dare let white people know that you could read, in those days. I remember one colored man, Alfred Evans, who used to read the Bible during slavery time. (Mary Colbert, Georgia)[22]

The white folks did not allow us to have nothing to do with books. You better not be found trying to learn to read. Our master was harder down on that than anything else. You better not be caught with a book. They read the Bible and told us to obey our masters for the Bible said obey your master. (Hannah Crasson, North Carolina)[23]

No, they were cut off from education. The way my stepfather got his learning was a colored blacksmith who would teach school at night, and us children taught our mother. She didn't know how to spell or read nothing. She didn't know B from the bull's foot. Some of them were allowed to have church and some didn't. Mighty few read the Bible 'cause they couldn't read. As my mother used to say, they were raised up green as cucumbers. (Julia Blanks, Texas)[24]

"Why are they so hellbent on being religious if they're just going to ignore everything the book says?" Sister asked. "What's the point?"

"The parts they like go a mighty long way to excusing how they treat us," said the preacher.

Sister puzzled on that for a moment. The old man gave her the time, eyes twinkling.

"So the kind of Christianity Marse and Missus talk about . . . that's something different from what we're talking about here?"

"I tell you what," said the preacher. "You just keep on reading that Good Book, Sister, and you tell me who looks more like Christ: Cook or Missus. And when you stumble upon that answer, you just let me know."

"AND HIM CLAIMING TO BE SUCH A CHRISTIAN!"

But they never dispute none with their brother about how mean he treat his slaves. And him claiming to be such a Christian! Well, I reckon he's found out something about slave driving by now. The good Lord has to get his work in some time. And he'll take care of them low-down Pattyroolers and slave speculators and mean Marsters and Mistresses. He's took good care of me in the years since I was freed, only now, we needs him again now and then. I just stand up on my two feet, raise my arms to heaven, and say, "Lord, help me!" He never fails me. I asked him this morning, didn't I Lola? Asked him to render help. We need it. And here you come. (Robert Falls, Tennessee)[25]

I seen old Master get mad at Truman and he buckled him down across a barrel and whupped him till he cut the blood out of him and then he rubbed salt and pepper in the raw places. It looked like Truman would die it hurt so bad. I know that don't sound reasonable that a white man in a Christian community would do such a thing but you can't realize how heartless he was. (Annie Hawkins, Oklahoma)[26]

They could have prayer meetings all they wanted to, but instructions from the Bible were thought dangerous for slaves. He did not wish them to become too wise and get it into their heads to run away and get free. (Randall Lee, Florida)[27]

Ring Shout

They told her that the ring shout came from Africa.

That the way they shuffled their feet, clapped their hands, and sang in unison came from the motherland. That it was how they'd worshiped then and how they'd grown to worship now. The way they shifted from claps and sways to holding up their skirts in one hand and cradling their hip in the other, whooping, yipping, shouting, dancing, praying—they brought that from home.

Sister didn't participate at first. She stood off to the side, clapping out the rhythm of their praise, nodding along to the songs she'd heard others sing. She watched her boys moving more comfortably in the throng of worshipers, clapping and stomping and smiling with zeal.

Then one night, down in the hollow, they sang a song Sister hadn't heard before, one she must have missed in all her ducking and dodging of these little worship services. She'd been sneaking into the study again just as she had when she was a child, reading the Bible this time instead of *The Iliad*. She'd been reading the prophets, of all people, and learning about the Savior they promised. The One who hated oppression and unfairness and decimated entire nations because of their sin toward other people—even his own nation of Israel.

The Savior they promised sounded so different from the one Sister had always imagined. And as she read those prophets, aching and waiting for their Savior to come and make all of the pain right, she felt that maybe she understood a bit of what they'd been feeling, waiting for the day to break.

Pastor had brought this new song with him from Georgia, where he'd worked in the Sea Islands with the Gullah people. He stood there, stomping and clapping out an insistent beat as he taught them the words in his husky tenor, frayed and threadbare around the edges.

After he sang it through once, he pulled Sister into the circle and told her when to say, "Yonder come day." She was shy at first, but it was dark enough in the moonlight that she could barely make out the whites of the eyes peering back at her.

"Yonder come day," they started.

"Day is a-breaking!" he sang.

"Yonder come day," she answered.

"Oh my soul."

"Yonder come day," she said again.

"Day is a-breaking, sun is a-rising in my soul."

> Sun rise, sun rise, oh yonder
> Yonder come day,
> Day is a-breaking
> Yonder come day,
> Oh my soul.

The insistent clapping of everyone around them coalesced into a rhythm Sister found with her feet, eyes shut, hands clapping, three words on her tongue: "Yonder come day."

Yonder Come Day

This night she was living through could come to an end.

> Yonder come day.
> Day could break.
> Yonder come day.
> Freedom could find her.

She sang and moved and clapped and cried without a hint of embarrassment then, tears running down her cheeks. Nothing had materially changed in that moment. One child had been sold away, another had died, she didn't know where her husband was, she'd never see her mother again, and freedom might be coming or it might not. But the hope in the words became buried deep in her heart as she sang them in rhythm with the tambourine and the washboard, her feet keeping time like the drums of the homeland that some of the gathered remembered.

By the time the song ended, she was bent double, sobbing. The preacher patted her shoulder. “Day is breaking,” he whispered. “Sun is rising.”

Yonder come day.

COLLECTIVE WITNESS: JAMES’S STORY

James Smith was sixteen years old when he consulted his enslaver, William Wright, about the possibility of being baptized. Wright, described by James later as a “hard master,” consented to the baptism, provided James passed the following examination:

> Do you feel as if you loved your master better than you ever did before, and if you could do more work and do it better?
>
> Do you feel willing to bear correction when it is given you, like a good and faithful servant, without fretting, murmuring, or running away as has heretofore been your practice?
>
> If so, it is an evidence that you are a good boy, and you may be baptized.

After his baptism, James felt called to “labor for the salvation of souls” and spent his time evangelizing those enslaved alongside him. However, Wright had consented to the baptism but not to having a slave who might be seen as an agitator.

So, many Sundays, he took to tying James up so that he wouldn’t go out and try to preach on his day off. Other Sundays, he would flog James “until his blood would drip down at his feet.” Still, James was undaunted. He continued to share the gospel as he understood it, one very different from the truncated version he had agreed to in order to be baptized.

In retaliation, William Wright sold James away from his wife and two young children.

James's former enslaver reported that there was "but one fault in this boy," despite his trustworthiness, faithfulness, and work ethic:

> He would run about at nights and on Sundays trying to preach the gospel among the slave population, which had a tendency to divert their attention from their work, and made them dissatisfied also, and that he had frequently flogged him with a rough hide until his back was literally bathed with blood, yet he'd slip off and do the same thing over again.

The new master was undaunted by these details: "I can soon break him of that practice." Upon departing his family, James remembered that "at that moment it seemed as if my poor heart would break with grief":

> After pressing his little ones to his breast, he kneeled down and commended them to the God of heaven; but before these religious exercises were concluded, he was driven from his knees by the stern voice of the driver, who brought the handcuffs, and locked them about his wrists. Under the most afflicting trial his wife seemed to bear up with Christian fortitude striving to console her husband and pleading herself to meet him in a better world than this.

His new slaveholder had rules against all religious meetings, which James soon broke by singing and praying in the small cabin where he lived with ten other slaves. When this infraction was reported to the overseer, James was told that if he promised to stop praying, he could avoid punishment.

James replied he "could never pledge himself to refrain from praying, though his life should be taken."

"For this expression," James said later, "I was most unmercifully bruised and mangled."

This abuse continued for James Smith, sometimes at the hands of those who had no patience for his religious fervor and other times as part of the ever-present suffering inherent to a life in slavery.

Eventually, James ran away and made his way to Canada. Shortly after his arrival, James heard about a woman who had once belonged to a man named William Wright. It had been seventeen years since James was sold away from his wife and young children, and he was anxious to see who this woman might be.

Miraculously, it was, indeed, his wife:

> At this moment her eyes sparkled and flashed like strokes of lightning upon his furrowed cheeks and wrinkled brow, and with uplifted hands and joyful heart she exclaimed from the depths of her soul, "Oh! Is this my beloved husband who I never again expected to see?"

She'd escaped from bondage as well, after watching their two children "scattered and sold apart."[28]

This story ostensibly starts with two Christians. One, William Wright, was a member of a local Baptist church. The other, James Smith, was his slave.

One Christian owned several people.

The other was owned, and even his baptism had to be done at the whim of his enslaver.

One Christian thought that preaching the gospel was a distraction from day-to-day work.

The other could not be silent about all that the Lord had done.

One Christian sold a husband away from his family and two children away from their mother.

The other was bought and sold several times because his religious fervor was an inconvenience to his enslavers.

William Wright was, according to himself, a Christian who played a vital role in driving a permanent wedge between a fellow Christian and his children.

James's story is not that of a man who was forced into Christianity but of one whose enslavers would've found it a lot more convenient had he answered only to them and not to God. James had a faith he wanted to shout from the rooftops; Wright had a faith that was compartmentalized from his treatment of other people who were made in the image of God.

As the preacher might've asked Sister, Whose faith looked more like Jesus?

CHAPTER 8

Dove

It was the plan of God to free us, and not Abraham Lincoln's.

George Strickland, Florida

Abraham Lincoln freed us by the help of the Lord, by his help.

Louisa Adams, North Carolina

We knowed freedom was on us, but we didn't know what was to come along with it. We thought we was going to get rich like white folks.

Felix Haywood, Texas

The whispers of freedom had been making their way across every plantation in the Delta.

The Battle of Vicksburg took place just one hundred miles away from the plantation, and the Union's victory seemed imminent. Sister had still been stealing every bit of news she could from the papers in the Big House, and in January 1863, she cut out a piece of the *Natchez Daily Courier*:

So far as the South is concerned, the Lincoln Emancipation Proclamation needs very little discussion. Its blighting and deadly

> objects have long since been made known to us through the Abolition journals of the North. This is not the time for discussion; it is the hour for action. If a man in your own country sets fire to your residence, thereby endangering lives, you hang him. If he murders your kinsman, you hang him. If he is an aider and abetter, you hang him or put him out of the way. If Lincoln's commissioned scoundrels come among us for the same diabolical purposes, why, hang them, and string them to the first tree, that those whom they would endeavor to corrupt may witness their terrible fate. The day has passed for argument; the hour has come for quick retribution on the heads of the invaders.[1]

There was some more about hanging the Union's commissioned officers and letting "their uncouth bodies die and rot as high as Haman's did," but Sister's eyes homed in on the words "Emancipation Proclamation." From what she could gather in the other papers she snatched, this proclamation was supposed to free all slaves. Though she hadn't felt any of that freedom, the *Courier* seemed to suggest that other people had:

> The Emancipation Proclamation is already working its results at Norfolk; slaves are becoming worthless, insolent and impudent, and owners are imprisoned when they chastise them.[2]

She explained all she could at their meetings in the hollow, but she was met with more questions than she had answers for.

"SHE WOULD STEAL THE NEWSPAPERS"

The Crawford children were caught teaching my mother to read and write, but they were made to stop. Mother was quick to learn and she never gave up. She would steal the newspapers and read up about the war, and she kept the other slaves posted as to how the war was progressing. She knew when the war was over, almost as soon as Marse John did. (Minnie Davis, Georgia)[3]

My grandma used to steal newspapers out of his house and take them down to the quarters and leave them there where there were one or two slaves that could read and tell how the War was goin' on. I never did learn how the slaves learned to read. But she was in the house and she could steal the papers and send them down. Later she could slip off and they would tell her the news, and then she could slip the papers back. (Victoria McMullen, Arkansas)[4]

In them days you better not be caught with a newspaper, else you got a beating and your back almost cut off. (Alice Douglass, Oklahoma)[5]

Relating an incident after having learned to read and write, one day as he was reading a newspaper, the master walked upon him unexpectedly and demanded to know what he was doing with a newspaper. He immediately turned the paper upside down and declared "Confederates done won the war." The master laughed and walked away without punishing him. It is interesting to know that slaves on this plantation were not allowed to sing when they were at work, but with all the vigilance of the overseers, nothing could stop those silent songs of labor and prayers for freedom. (Squires Jackson, Florida)[6]

Along with the news of the Yankees' advance came the unwelcome news of many Southern families fleeing to Texas as refugees. Sister had gotten word that Sun's master and missus had taken him to Texas several weeks ago. She had no more tears to cry, but she watched as other wives, sisters, and daughters mourned further separation from their families. "They say if you go to Texas, you'll never get free."

"WE WAS REFUGEES"

"Refugees" refers to Confederate families who fled from the advance of the Union. Many of them ended up in Texas, which was seen as the state that would be the last holdout against the Union effort.

We was refugees. Boles, our master, sent us out and we come from Holmes County to Cherokee County in a wagon. We was a dodging in and out, running from the Yankees. Marster said they was running us from the Yankees to keep us, but we was free and didn't know it. (Elvira Boles, Texas)[7]

The fighting was not close enough to make trouble. Jus' 'fore freedom come, the new overseer am instructed to take us to Texas and takes us to Kaufman County and we is refugees there. (Fred Brown, Texas)[8]

Cotton was a good price then and them slave buyers had plenty of money. We was sold to Jim Ingram, of Carthage. He bought a big gang of slaves and refugeed part of 'em to Louisiana and part to Texas. We come to Texas in ox wagons. (Wash Ingram, Texas)[9]

The familiar helplessness gripped Sister's heart. At least she could steal newspapers—others were kept completely in the dark as masters like hers hid news of the Emancipation Proclamation from them.

Outside of the prohibited newspaper readings, word traveled slower among the enslaved than among the white folks, carried from plantation to plantation on visiting days until it finally made it to them months later. They'd found through the grapevine that some slaves who lived near Union camps had escaped and found sanctuary among Yankee soldiers.

They called these places "contraband camps," Sister had read, and she learned by word of mouth there was one in Corinth, Mississippi.

Corinth was a good two hundred miles away from her plantation, and Sister had her sons to think about. She knew that some mothers had counted the cost and fled, leaving their young children behind, but with Sun and one daughter gone, she could not imagine further fracturing the family she still had left.

COLLECTIVE WITNESS: STAYING CONTRABAND

"Do you want to know how I runned away and joined the Yankees?" ninety-eight-year-old Boston Blackwell asked his interviewer, Beulah Sherwood Hagg, in Arkansas.[10]

Beulah must have answered in the affirmative, because Boston launched into a story that started with Abraham Lincoln's declaration of freedom on the first day of January, 1863. Boston didn't run away then, though. He bided his time for a few more months, perhaps waiting until he could form a plan of escape.

Several of the elderly WPA interviewees recalled hearing about their freedom before they were allowed to act upon it. Still others were kept in the dark about their emancipation for as long as possible. In October 1863, though, with full knowledge of the rights the Emancipation Proclamation had conferred, Boston got into trouble with his overseer. Before he could be whipped, he told his sister, "I'se leaving this here place for good."

His sister cried and said, "Overseer man, he will kill you."

Boston remembered, "I says, 'He kill me anyhow.'"

He left with another young, enslaved man named Jerry. They could hear the hounds "a-howling, getting ready for to chase after" them, but they "hide in dark woods." That October night was incredibly cold in Arkansas, and Jerry wanted to give up several times along the way, but Boston wouldn't let him.

Eventually, they made their way to Pine Bluff, an abandoned farm turned makeshift contraband settlement.

Boston described the sight:

> When we gets to the Yankee camp all our troubles was over. We gets all the contraband we could eat. Was they more runaways there? Oh, Lordy, yessum. Hundred, I reckon. Yessum, the Yankees feeds all them refugees on contraband. They made me a driver of a team in the quartermasters department. I was always careful to do everything they telled me. They telled me I was free when I gets to the Yankee camp, but I couldn't go outside much.

> Yessum, iffen you could get to the Yankee camp you was free right now.

The Emancipation Proclamation didn't free Boston Blackwell—he freed himself.

Boston Blackwell and so many others waited on the plantations where their freedom had supposedly been declared. In many cases, their freedom was not recognized by their enslavers and not extended to them in full until after the Civil War's end.

But that didn't stop Boston Blackwell and others from laying claim to freedom for themselves.

As the Union soldiers began making inroads into the South, the enslaved started pouring into their camps by the thousands, even in the years before the Emancipation Proclamation was issued. At first, there was no policy in place to deal with these formerly enslaved refugees who sought the protection of Union soldiers.

Some commanders put them to work for Union troops, as Boston experienced, but others returned them to the plantation owners they'd fled. In 1861, at Fort Monroe in Hampton, Virginia, Union Major General Benjamin Butler refused to send three fugitives back into the bonds of slavery. He classified escaping slaves as contraband of war.

Following Butler's actions, federal policy was instituted on August 6, 1861, officially declaring the fugitives "contraband of war" if their labor had been used to aid the Confederacy in any way. If found to be contraband, they were declared free.

The contraband camps teemed with new additions after the Emancipation Proclamation, and the refugees proved valuable to the Union, particularly as future soldiers—once Lincoln lifted the ban on Black participation. The formerly enslaved injected the Union with the manpower it needed to continue the fight.

Following the proclamation, almost 200,000 Black men joined the Union Army and Navy. But in so many ways, the proclamation merely made official what was already occurring.

W. E. B. Du Bois described it this way:

> With perplexed and laggard steps, the United States Government followed the footsteps of the black slave toward freedom.[11]

The abolition of slavery was not the inevitable outcome of the Civil War from the first shot fired, nor was the solidification of Black citizenship. It was through the self-advocacy of young people like Boston that freedom became the central object of the war. The South fought to preserve slavery, the North fought to preserve the Union, and the enslaved fought for their freedom.

> When the soldier wagons came down to get the feed, they would take one crib and leave one. They never bothered the smokehouse. They took all the dry cattle to feed the people that were contrabands. But they left the milk cows. The quartermaster for the contrabands was Captain Mallory. The contrabands were mostly slaves that they kept in camps just below Pine Bluff for their own protection.[12]

For many, contraband camps offered the first taste of freedom. Though often overcrowded and disorganized, they became places of respite for the formerly enslaved to experience new levels of independence. Teachers began to arrive from the North, setting up schools for children and adults alike. Men and women worked to provide for their families and gain sea legs as free citizens of a changing country.

"THE PEOPLE WHEREOF SHALL THEN BE IN REBELLION"

When Abraham Lincoln issued the proclamation, it freed "all persons held as slaves within any State" that was "in rebellion" against the United States. So, in reality, it did not free the enslaved in the border states or Union-occupied states. And it was not heeded by the Confederate states that rebelled against the Union to preserve this very "peculiar institution."

Sister's understanding of the Emancipation Proclamation was as limited as much of the general public's is today. She, like so many others, took Lincoln's proclamation to mean that all enslaved people in all territories in America were now free. However, in reality, the proclamation had limits: "All persons held as slaves within any State or designated part of a State, the people whereof shall then be in rebellion against the United States, shall be then, thenceforward, and forever free."[13]

Maryland, Delaware, Kentucky, and Missouri were all slaveholding states that were part of the Union. Each had battled it out to decide whether they would join the Confederacy, but, ultimately, the Union kept control. Therefore, the proclamation did not apply to the enslaved within their borders. Portions of formerly Confederate states were also exempt from the proclamation because they'd been brought under Union control.

The proclamation only applied to the Carolinas, Mississippi, Florida, Alabama, Georgia, Texas, and Arkansas—Confederate states that refused to recognize Lincoln's authority to pass the act.

William Seward, Lincoln's Secretary of State, commented, "We show our sympathy with slavery by emancipating slaves where we cannot reach them and holding them in bondage where we can set them free."[14]

Staying Home

Sister did not go to the contraband camp at Corinth. She stayed put, hoping and praying that, by doing so, Sun would be able to find her. And so, together, she and her children waited for the freedom that had been declared to come and find them on the plantation.

And eventually, it did.

By the time Marse gathered his slaves in the side yard, some folks had already made their way to Corinth and beyond. Rations had been cut in half because of the fighting. Yankees had been spotted at nearby farms. Missy's husband had died at Vicksburg, and Marse increased the number of sales as he saw the writing on the wall, realizing that his human property would not have value, or be his property, much longer.

Hypocritically, his buying and trading in human flesh did not stop him from playing the part of the benevolent patriarch when he stood before them to tell them the war was over.

"You're free now," he said. "Just as free as I am. But you're welcome to stay here until you can get on your feet."

He meant, "You're welcome to stay here until you harvest the crops," and almost everyone knew that. But only a few people decided to leave at first, mostly because they didn't know where to go. Some, like Sister, had families they wanted to find or wait for. Others were afraid of the violence they'd heard befell the formerly enslaved who made their way from plantations into the wide world beyond.

Sister decided that she and her sons would stay on for three more months. By that time, if they hadn't been found by Sun, they would make their way North. Where to, she did not know, but they couldn't stay here forever.

"THE GOVERNMENT DON'T NEED TO TELL YOU YOU IS FREE"

My father told us when freedom come. He'd been a free man, 'cause he was bodyguard to the old, old master and when he died he give my father he freedom. That was over in Richmond, Virginia. But young master steal him into slavery again. So he was glad when freedom come and he was free again. (Carey Davenport, Texas)[15]

One morning, Papa Day calls us to the house and reads the freedom papers and say, "The government don't need to tell you you is free, 'cause you been free all you days. If you wants to stay you can and if you wants to go, you can. But if you go, lots of white folks ain't going treat you like I does." (Laura Cornish, Texas)[16]

> We knowed freedom was on us, but we didn't know what was to come with it. We thought we was goin' to get rich like the white folks. We thought we was goin' to be richer than the white folks, 'cause we was stronger and knowed how to work, and the whites didn't and they didn't have us to work for them anymore. But it didn't turn out that way. We soon found out that freedom could make folks proud but it didn't make 'em rich. (Felix Haywood, Texas)[17]

COLLECTIVE WITNESS: HOLDING ON

Malindy Maxwell was born near Como and Sardis, Mississippi.

Her mother and father were owned by two different enslavers—the Shans family and the Sanders family. Though neither enslaver would sell their property, they allowed Malindy's parents to marry one another and enjoy a proper wedding at that. The couple had a big supper, a preacher presided over the ceremony, and the bride wore white.

Malindy's mother and father had seven children together and were fortunate enough to keep their family from being torn asunder in the years leading up to emancipation. As soon as they were free, "Pa went to see about marrying Ma over again." He wanted a marriage that would stand "long as ever he lived."[18]

It was a new hope that could live in a post-emancipation world—one that the formerly enslaved would not take for granted:

> On May 30, 1865, Maj. Gen. Oliver Otis Howard, who was appointed by President Andrew Johnson as commissioner of newly formed Freedmen's Bureau, issued orders to his assistant commissioners—who were responsible for the daily operations of the bureau in the former Confederate states, Border States, and the District of Columbia—on the conditions for solemnizing former slave marriages. Continuing the practice started by military and civilian officials at government camps, Howard told his subordinates, "In places where the local statutes make no provisions for

> the marriage of persons of color, the assistant commissioners are authorized to designate officers who shall keep a record of marriages, which may be solemnized by any ordained minister of the gospel." Howard's orders also required ministers to report on marriages they performed, including "such items as may be required for registration at places designated by assistant commissioners." Marriages that had been already recorded by military officers were to be preserved.[19]

Other formerly slaveholding states followed suit, offering avenues to formally legalize the marriages of the formerly enslaved. But so many of those marriages had already been legitimate in the eyes of husbands, wives, and children for whom a lifelong connection to one another was often tenuous.

Roughly half of all enslaved people were separated from their spouses and parents.

The miracle of Malindy's family remaining whole through the end of slavery was not a common one. And yet, others still married for love despite the inherent risks. They still bore children and had families. Yes, they often did so because their masters bade it, but they also did it for the love of their spouses and their children. And, in slavery, love was always a risk.

It was a risk that so many kept taking.

COLLECTIVE WITNESS: REUNION

For so many, freedom meant an opportunity to be reunited with family members they'd lost during the heyday of the slave trade. Not every story had a happy ending, but enough did to bolster the hopes of those who kept seeking their loved ones, even when it seemed impossible to find them.

> CARROLLTON, Ky., Nov. 27.—Alexander Foley of Natchez, Miss., a former slave, arrived here a few days ago to visit Dr. Goslie, who

> used to be his old master. His surprise could be imagined when he was told by Dr. Goslie that his wife, who was sold from him forty years ago, was living in Carrollton.[20]

> SHELBYVILLE, Tenn., Sept. 24.—A somewhat romantic marriage occurred in colored circles last night. The facts about it are these: Before the Civil War, and in slave times, Jeff Frierson, a slave belonging to the Friersons of this county, and Mary Burt, a slave belonging to Thomas Burt, lived together as man and wife under the old slave system of marriage. But a few years before the Civil War Mr. Burt sold Mary to an Arkansas man, who took her to that State, and there she has since resided, while Jeff still remained here.
>
> A few days ago, however, Mary returned here on a visit to some of her relatives. Soon after her arrival she happened to meet Jeff, her one-time husband, whom she thought was long since dead.[21]

These sweet reunions, facilitated through ads in newspapers and word of mouth, were not always possible. Again and again, the formerly enslaved interviewed by the WPA recounted being separated from mothers, fathers, husbands, wives, and siblings, never to see or hear from them "in this life or the next."

For a reunion to occur, there had to be some measure of knowledge. The enslaved would need to remember faces and names—surnames of enslavers if not the surnames of those whom they sought. They had to follow the trail of people who were often sold multiple times throughout their lives. They had to persist even after that trail went cold.

Young children who were sold away from their mothers might never have learned a name, might never remember a face, might walk by their mother one day without even realizing who the woman was, so unfamiliar would they be with the woman who bore them. Mothers who had lost young children might search every face they passed that seemed the right age, looked like they could be related, or reminded them of the children they had lost:

> POWERS, Mich.—Solomon Terry, an ex-slave and well-known character, who was almost 100 years old, was found near the Cedar River Land company's camp No. 8, sitting near a logging road. He was taken to the camp and died on Monday from a stroke of paralysis. He was born in Tennessee and was a slave for about ten years. He was married when a young man and one child resulted from the union. Later he was forced to witness the sale of his wife and child. The wife was bought by one master and the child by another, and the home was broken up, and Terry never saw or heard of either since.[22]

And yet, so many parents refused to give up hope:

> DEAR EDITOR—I wish to inquire as to the whereabouts of my daughter Kittie, whom I left with her mother, Hettie, in Tallahatchie Co., Mississippi, three miles from Oakville in 1850. Kitty was the only child when I left there. I came away with Nathan Reed. If she is living she will be 31 years of age this coming August. I left them with one Moses Peterson. I heard after I left there that her mother married one Jim Jones. Her mother had one sister named Kittie, who lived with one Darby, in Yalabusha Co., near Oakville. Please address me at Prairie Lea, Caldwell Co., Texas.[23]

And for some parents, that hope came to fruition. Miraculous tales of reunion were circulated in local newspapers for all to see with headlines like, "Mrs. Anna Mollie Wright Reunited with Her Daughter Mrs. Anna Freeman after 29 Years,"[24] "Hiram Jefferson Reunited with Son Thomas after 30 Years,"[25] and "Unidentified Parents Reunited with Their Daughter after 20 Years."[26]

These reunion stories bolstered the hopes of many who would never know reunions of their own.

Dove

Sister's time on the plantation had come to a close.

She and her boys were ready to strike out for freedom, whatever that meant. It did not feel right to keep living on the plantation where so much grief had hunted her, where the memories of her lost children and stolen husband haunted every waking day. The three months she'd allotted had passed, along with the harvest, and plenty of others were making their way out into the world to see what freedom would mean in the land beyond.

Sister packed up her meager possessions, including all of the quilts she had made during her time here—from the first stuttering attempt under Cook's tutelage to the latest, most beautiful quilt she'd ever made, finally using Mama's cloth. They told the story she was still stitching with her sons.

She led her three children out of their ramshackle cabin—the place she had made their home. It looked so small and weather-beaten to her now that she could imagine a different kind of home, one built of love and not of bare utility. One that would be her very own.

Her boys were in high spirits, excited for the adventure ahead. Sister hid her worry from them, trying to keep a brave face for the boys who would meet their brand-new freedom full of smiles and hope. She was bound and determined to create the life for them that they deserved, one that involved more than nighttime reading lessons by the smoldering embers of a hidden fire. Her children could be anything they wanted to be in this vast new frontier, she thought. And her family could be whole in a new way.

They weren't alone when they set out on the road into town. A few other formerly enslaved families walked alongside them, heading toward the nearest contraband camp turned freedman's colony in hopes that the northern missionaries who had been sent to the war-torn South in the war's wake would be able to help them get a solid start. She'd heard of the Freedmen's Bureau helping freed men and women find jobs, lodging, and even loans.

Sister tried to hustle her boys along the road, but they gawked, wide-eyed, at everything they passed. They had never left the boundaries of the plantation where they'd been born, and every new sight held wonder. Their world was so small, Sister realized, as she, too, marveled at the town they passed through. Freedom was expanding their scope minute by minute.

"Don't dawdle," she kept telling them. "Don't wander. Eyes ahead."

One of her sons was so distracted by something ahead that he started walking quickly toward the sight. Sister called after him in frustration, trying to balance her bag on her shoulder and keep hold of her youngest son's hand.

When she caught up with him, she would give him a piece of her mind. The boy was dumbfounded, of course, but so were they all. He would have to learn to control his impulses in this wide new world. He would have to learn to . . .

Sister saw what, or rather *who*, he had been running toward.

A tall, broad-shouldered man with laughing eyes scooped the gangly boy up as though he were a little child, laughing as he spun him around in a triumphant circle.

Sister dropped her bag.

Her other sons ran toward the man now, smiling, laughing, calling out to him.

Sister stared, mouth agape, mind trying to make sense of what she was seeing.

The man looked toward her and smiled a dazzling, brilliant, sunshine glow that took her breath away.

Sun.

Sister had been free for three months now, even longer if she counted back to Lincoln's Emancipation Proclamation. Slavery as she'd always known it had been abolished in the South, and she was a woman made new in liberty. But it wasn't until she ran into her husband's arms, tears streaming down her face as her sons gathered around them laughing and whooping and clamoring, that she tasted true freedom.

The freedom to love them all without fear they would be snatched away had not felt real until this moment. Their new version of family—their new version of wholeness—expanded again to include the father they had been waiting for. And though her boys would never find the sisters they had lost—one in heaven and one out in this wide new world, hopefully being cherished by a found family of her own—they would never let each other go again.

If Sister had chosen a free name, it would have been Dove, the bird Noah sent out of the ark in hopeful search of a dry place to land. That dove was a seeker, and it kept seeking until it found what it was looking for . . . and then it never came back again.

Dove would never turn back from the peace she'd found in that moment with her family. No matter where they went or what they did for work, they were together, and they were free. And she would spend the rest of her life fighting to keep that peace safe and sacred in her newfound freedom.

COLLECTIVE WITNESS: A DIFFERENT ENDING

Freedom did not always bring harmonious reunions between spouses, even when they were able to find one another. In the ever-shifting economy of slavery, families were often torn asunder and made anew in ways far outside the control of the enslaved and the emancipated.

"Aunt Sally" Graves recalled her own separation from her father:

> We left my papa in Kentucky, 'cause he was allotted to another man. My papa never knew where my mama went, and my mama never knew where papa went. They never wanted mama to know, 'cause they knowed she would never marry so long she knew where he was. Our master wanted her to marry again and raise more children to be slaves. They never wanted mama to know where papa was, an' she never did.

Sally went on:

> Mama said she would never marry again to have children, so she married my stepfather, Trattle Barber, 'cause he was sick and could never be a father. He was so sick he couldn't work, so me and mama had to work hard. (Sarah Frances Shaw Graves, Missouri)[27]

Sally's mama was forced to marry again, as was so often the nature of an enslaved woman's tenuous autonomy. She was at least able to make the choice not to start a new family, but others were not able to achieve such maneuvers. Virginia Bell of Texas remembered:

> I know my pappy is a lot older than my mother and he had a wife and five children back in Virginia and had been sold away from them back there. (Virginia Bell, Texas)[28]

If Virginia's pappy had ever been reunited with his first wife, he would have been in a woeful conundrum for marrying again, even though he was likely forced to do so by his enslaver. Chances were, though, that the man never did see his first wife and five children again, and his first wife was likely forced to start a new family as well once he had been sold.

After the war, one piece of Mississippi legislation brought the lack of sanctity viewed in slave marriages into sharp relief:

> Our laws recognize no marital rights as between slaves; their sexual intercourse is left to be regulated by their owners. The regulations of law, as to the white race, on the subject of sexual intercourse, do not and cannot, for obvious reasons, apply to slaves; their intercourse is promiscuous.[29]

According to the law, the marriage and intercourse of the enslaved was seen merely as a tool for procreation and control. Therefore, the moment it stopped being profitable for the enslaver, it ceased to be protected by law or custom. Virginia's and Sally's parents were both slotted into new unions as though their past relationships had never existed.

After emancipation, some formerly married enslaved couples started families with new partners because they never hoped to find their spouses again, or if they did find them, they assumed they might have started new families in the same fashion as Virginia's father.

Laura Spicer and her young children were sold away from her husband during slavery. After emancipation, they found one another, but her husband had already remarried. Their letters reveal the pain and complexity of their separation.

Laura wrote, "I read your letters over and over again. I keep them always in my pocket. If you are married, I don't ever want to see you again."

Her former husband replied:

> I would much rather you would get married to some good man, for every time I gits a letter from you it tears me all to pieces. The reason why I have not written you before, in a long time, is because your letters disturbed me so very much. You know I love my children. I treats them good as a Father can treat his children; and I do a good deal of it for you. I am sorry to hear that Lewellyn, my poor little son, have had such bad health. I would come and see you but I know you could not bear it. I want to see and I don't want to see you. I love you just as well as I did the last day I saw you, and it will not do for you and I to meet. I am married, and my wife have two children, and if you and I meets it would make a very dissatisfied family.

He asked her to send him "some of my children's hair, in a separate paper with their names on the paper," and told her, "the woman is not born that feels as near to me as you do. You feel this day like myself. . . . Laura, I do love you the same. My love to you *never* have failed."

His turmoil was palpable. Clearly, he felt a duty to his new wife and children, such that he begged Laura to remarry as well, telling her that he could not see her for fear of upsetting his new family. But again and again, he returned to the truth of his love for Laura. "I have got another wife, and I am very sorry, that I am. You feels and seems to me as much like my dear loving wife, as you ever did Laura."[30]

More than once, stories of reunions happened later in life, after new spouses had passed away. This was the case for Alexander Foley and his wife, who were reunited after forty years apart. Alexander's second wife had died, leaving him free to reunite with his first wife, a woman whom he had been married to for a much shorter period of time before she was sold away.[31] Milton Douglas and his wife were also separated as newlyweds during slavery—Mrs. Douglas remarried but was reunited with Milton after her husband had died.[32]

Often, the formerly enslaved embarked upon their new life with new versions of the family life they had known in slavery. There were missing pieces—spouses, children, parents, siblings—and sometimes those pieces were never recovered. Other times, those pieces were found but never fit in the same way again. And still other times, those pieces were reshaped to fit in brand-new ways.

In emancipation, the formerly enslaved had the freedom to discover just how those puzzle pieces could come together again. For many, that decision was the first step into freedom.

INTERLUDE

Samuel Shinkle Taylor[1]

Samuel Shinkle Taylor brought his daughter, Yvonne, with him to many of his interviews for the Works Progress Administration.

Arkansas was responsible for about a third of the interviews collected by the WPA, and Taylor conducted about 17 percent of those interviews. He was well-known to the Black community of Little Rock, Arkansas, having moved there in 1927 to become the head of the Department of Education and of Philander Smith College from 1927 to 1929 before transitioning to teach math at Dunbar Junior High School.

A veteran of the Great War, Taylor was a lifelong educator and a thorough interviewer. Where other interviewers provided little context for their subjects, Taylor took his time. He reported whether or not his interviewees seemed comfortable or hesitant to talk to him. He went above and beyond by fact-checking ages and other details the interviewees offered. He even provided helpful headings throughout his interviews to help guide the topics being discussed.

Taylor was one of two Black Arkansas fieldworkers. It's been noted that throughout the project, Black interviewers tended to pull out more intense reckonings than their white counterparts. The reasons for this are manifold:

A lot of the interviewers were white women who were interviewing Black men in the Jim Crow South. Their interaction represented a host of social hierarchies and dangers for those men.

A lot of the interviewees *knew* their interviewers. In some cases, interviewees had either been enslaved by their families or knew their families were former enslavers.

A lot of interviewees were hungry and on flimsy relief benefits that left them both vulnerable to the charity of their interviewers and more likely to opine about the "good old days" of slavery. For instance, many interviewees remembered that during slavery, they got to eat more than their Depression-era rations provided.

Renowned author Zora Neale Hurston, herself a WPA employee, captured one reason exceptionally well:

> Folklore is not as easy to collect as it sounds. The best source is where there are the least outside influences and these people, being usually underprivileged, are the shyest. They are most reluctant at times to reveal that which the soul lives by. And the Negro, in spite of his open-faced laughter, his seeming acquiescence, is particularly evasive. You see we are a polite people and we do not say to our questioner, "Get out of here!" We smile and tell him or her something that satisfies the white person because, knowing so little about us, he doesn't know what he is missing. The Indian resists curiosity by a stony silence. The Negro offers a feather-bed resistance. That is, we let the probe enter, but it never comes out. It gets smothered under a lot of laughter and pleasantries.[2]

Being a Black man, a pillar of the Little Rock community, and someone not afraid to ask probing questions even when he hit resistance served Taylor well. His connection to the subjects was clear in his extensive "interviewer's comments."

Upon hearing the story of Lucretia Alexander's rebellious father being sold five times for his unruliness and finally being bought to be reunited with Lucretia's mother, Samuel commented:

> I'll bet the grandest moment in the life of Sister Alexander's mother was when her mistress said, "Agnes, will you follow me if I buy your husband?" Fifteen hundred dollars to buy a rebellious slave in order to unite a slave couple. It's epic.[3]

Again, Taylor delights in an interviewee's stories in another comment on J. F. Boone's tale:

> If you have read this interview hastily and have missed the patroller joke on page three, turn back and read it now. The interviewer considers it the choicest thing in the story.[4]

When he encountered one crotchety subject, W. A. Anderson, who didn't much want to talk to him, Taylor pitched in around his home instead of leaving:

> I made three calls on him, helped him set up his stoves and his beds and clear up his house a little bit since he had just moved into it and had a good deal of work to do. His misfortunes have made him unwilling to talk just now, but he will give a good interview later I am certain.[5]

After interviewing Ellen Cragin, he was moved to compassion:

> There it was—the appeal to the slush fund. I have contributed to lunch, tobacco, and cold drinks, but not before to moving expenses. I had only six cents which I had reserved for car fare. But after you have talked with people who are too old to work, too feeble to help themselves in any effective fashion, hemmed up in a single room and unable to pay rent on that, odds and ends of broken and dilapidated furniture, ragged clothes, and not even plenty of water on hand for bathing, barely hanging on to the thread of

life without a thrill or a passion, then it is a great thing to have six cents to give away and to be able to walk any distance you want to.[6]

And rather than render his subjects in the hackneyed dialect as did his associates in other states, Taylor simply took note of the pronunciations after the fact:

This paper fails to record Fannie Dorum's accent with any approach to accuracy. She speaks fairly accurately and clearly and with a good deal of attention to grammaticalness. But she pronounces all "er" ending as "uh"; e.g., cullud, fathuh, mothuh, m(o)stuh, daughtuhs.

There are a number of variations from correct pronunciation which I do not record because they do not constitute a variation from the normal pronunciation; e.g., "wuz" for "was," "(e)r" for "[e]r."

The slave pronunciation of "m(o)ster" is more nearly correct than the normal pronunciation of "m(a)." Frequent pronunciations are marse, marsa, m(o)ssa, m(o)stuh, and m(a)ssa.[7]

Taylor brought out the dignity of those he interviewed, not just in the way he captured their language, but in the way he observed their understanding. Of Waters McIntosh, he reported:

Nothing is pleasanter than to view the relationship between him and his wife. They have been married fifty-six years and seem to have achieved a perfect understanding. She is an excellent cook and is devoted to her home. She attends church regularly. Seems to be four or five years younger than her husband. Like him, however, she seems to enjoy excellent health.[8]

After interviewing Amanda Ross, he wrote:

You can't get the whole story by reading the words in this interview. You have to hear the tones and the accents, and see the facial expressions and bodily movements, and sense the sometimes almost occult influence; you have to feel the utter lack of resentment that lies behind the words that sound vehement when read. You marvel at the quick, smooth cover-up when something is to be withheld, at the unexpected vigor of the mind when the bait is attractive enough to draw it out, and at the sweetness of the disposition. Some old people merely get mellowed and sweetened by the hardships through which they have passed. Sometimes, you wonder if some of the old folk don't have dispositions that they can turn off or on at will.

It is not hard to realize the reason why Amanda was treated better than other children when you remember that she called her grandpa "Master."[9]

He even noted when interviewees seemed stilted or odd in his presence, such as Martha Ruffin and Betty Johnson:

> The old lady's style was kind of cramped by the presence of her husband. Every once in a while, when she would be about to paint something in lurid colors, he would drop in a word and she would roll her phrases around in her mouth, so to speak, and shift and go ahead in a different direction and on another gear.[10]

> Betty Johnson's memory is accurate, and she tells whatever she wishes to tell without hesitation and clearly. She leaves out details which she does not wish to mention evidently, and there is a reserve in her manner which makes questioning beyond a certain point impertinent. However, just what she tells presents a picture into which the details may easily be fitted. . . .
>
> Although my questions traveled into corners where they evidently did not wish to follow, the mother and son, who was from time to time with her, answered courteously and showed no irritation.[11]

Given his thoroughness and intentionality, Taylor's interviews are highly regarded, standing out from not only his Arkansas compatriots but also the work of many of the other WPA interviewers.[12]

Historian John Blassingame praised Taylor as "the most skillful of the WPA interviewers," and George Rawick, who compiled and reintroduced the WPA slave narratives in 1972, refers to Taylor's interviews as "generally among the best in the collection."[13]

Taylor was set apart, not just by the fact that he was one of the rare Black interviewers in the field, or even by the fact that he was a known entity in Arkansas, but by his obvious compassion and care for his subjects. He wrote his interviews as though someone in the future might like to read them, providing as many details as possible in his notes, following up on important dates, setting the stage as best he could, and writing clearly and responsibly—not in the odd, minstrelsy-burdened dialect that so many other interviewers employed.

His secret weapon was likely the combination of a minister's heart, a teacher's attention to detail, and, perhaps, his daughter Yvonne.

Ms. Yvonne Frances Taylor Beatty made the following comment on the Encyclopedia of Arkansas website, where the most thorough online record of Samuel Taylor's life exists:

> I am the oldest of three surviving children of Samuel Shinkle Taylor. I was about twelve years old when he did the slave interviews and narratives. He taught me Gregg shorthand and often took me with him to help record the conversations. The interviewees would not speak freely if he wrote as he talked with them, and they assumed that I was just scribbling on a piece of paper.[14]

Taylor's care takes on even more texture when one imagines his twelve-year-old daughter sitting in the room with him and taking her notes. He was teasing out the stories that made up her legacy and the legacy she would pass down to her children. He was compiling these stories not just to fulfill a requirement for a white-collar job that fell into his lap during the New Deal but as a conscientious folklorist who took his position seriously.

Taylor wasn't the only interviewer to write asides. Alabamian and Georgian interviewers, in particular, loved to wax eloquent about their subjects.

Interviewer Alexander B. Johnson of Birmingham imagined after he spoke to Gus Brown:

> The reporter left him sitting with his little pack and a long fork in his hands; in his eyes, dimmed with age, a far-off look and a tear of longing for the Old Plantation. (Gus Brown, Alabama)[15]

J. Morgan Smith reported:

> When asked about slave days, he gets a far-away expression in his eyes; an expression of tranquil joy. (Simon Phillips, Alabama)[16]

Like Zoe Posey, other WPA interviewers were very interested in painting a specific picture of the old South, describing the men and women they interviewed as matronly or avuncular talismans of the good old days.

But for Taylor, the people he interviewed were, first, *people*—not props to support his vision of an idyllic old South. He had spent a life in service to others—as a husband, a father of five, a veteran, a minister, an administrator, a teacher, and now a folklorist—and his care for others came through in the way he handled the precious stories shared with him. When reading Taylor's interviews, one can't help but wonder what the three thousand testimonies that other interviewers gathered might look like if all had approached the project with the reverence with which it was due.

Was Yvonne with Taylor when he interviewed Sallie Crane? Did the young girl listen as Sallie told about being whipped "from sunup till sundown"? Did she hear Sallie talk about being gagged and bound for three days for trying to run away—how she was tied so tight that her slobber collected on her chest and attracted flies, and the maggots left scars where they'd eaten into her skin?

At the end of her interview, Sallie felt comfortable telling Samuel: "You gets 'round lots, son, don't you? Well; if you see anybody that has some old shoes they don't want, git 'em to give 'em to me."

And when she bid him farewell, Sallie said:

> You just come in any time; I can't talk to you like I would a woman; but I guess you can understand me. (Sallie Crane, Arkansas)[17]

What would the wealth of WPA interviews be like if everyone interviewed felt as at ease as Sallie Crane? Would there be as many reminiscences of "the good old days" performed for white interviewers by interviewees who knew exactly what they wanted to hear? Would there be more detailed notes, more readable transcripts, and more reliable witnesses?

The WPA Narratives still hold so much value, as I hope the stories collected here have shown. But they also hold a complexity that is highlighted by Samuel Shinkle Taylor's talent as a folklorist—a talent not shared by every interviewer who undertook the task of collecting these stories.

Something as simple as having a disarming little girl come with him to sit in the corner and take notes so that his hands could be free to hold the treasures he was being given by these elderly interviewees speaks volumes.

CHAPTER 9

Grandmama

The young people today! I'd hate to tell you what I do think of them. The business is going to fall.

Thomas Ruffin, Arkansas (age 82 or 84)

If the Lord lets you git back tomorrow, try and come a little sooner in the day than you did today. I gits up about six in the morning. I don't believe in layin' in bed late. I go to bed directly after dark and I wake up early. The Lord never did mean for nobody to sleep all day.

Laura Thornton, Arkansas (age 105)

I tries to do right. I am not perfect but I do the best I can. I ain't got no bottom teeth, but my top ones are good. I have a few bottom ones. The Lawd's keepin' me here for somethin'. I been with 'im now seventy-three years.

Lucretia Alexander, Arkansas (age 89)

I used to quilt until my fingers got too stiff. I got some patterns in there now if you want to see them.

Sarah Jane Patterson, Arkansas (age 90)

They always used to say that Grandmama was the oldest woman in Little Rock.

It was not a fact they'd ever proven.

A handful of other centenarians lived throughout Arkansas, along with plenty who might have fit the criteria if they knew their exact ages, but by her family's estimation, Grandmama exceeded them all at 112 years old. Her mind was still as sharp and agile as it had been back in her days as Little Bit, Lonely One, Lovely One, and every other iteration of her full life. And though the agility of her body had diminished, she made it a point to get up and walk to her mailbox every single day. Her eyesight had dimmed with age, but she wore thick Coke-bottle spectacles and held items two inches from her face, insistent upon her ability to read—which was still her pride and joy after all these years.

Grandmama had lived alone until her oldest great-granddaughter moved her from Mississippi to Arkansas so she could occupy their mother-in-law suite. She was still independent, sharing recipes in the kitchen that Cook taught her many years ago and tidying up what little dust her weathered eyes could see.

When the WPA field agent knocked on their door that afternoon, Granddaughter answered with a smile on her face. She'd known he was coming because they attended church together where Grandmama sat tall and proud in the front pew every single Sunday.

"Grandmama!" Granddaughter called into the house. "Someone's here to see you!"

Grandmama was sitting in the living room, holding a letter up to the light. It was sent by one of her fifty great-great-grandchildren, telling her something or other about Fisk University. She was able to make out most of it by herself, but Granddaughter would read it again to her this evening to make sure she'd soaked up every single detail.

Grandmama was different from the other interviewees this field agent had encountered. Most of them lived in the abject poverty characteristic of the Great Depression in this part of the country, occupying homes that were little more than lean-tos and putting up with shabby disrepair. Many field agents commented on the unsanitary conditions these elderly people occupied, as though an eighty-plus-year-old all alone in the world and beleaguered by poverty should be expected to maintain a pristine home when visited by an unexpected guest.

Granddaughter and her husband had good jobs, though, and they lived comfortably enough with their four children and Grandmama. So, unlike many of the other interviewees, when Grandmama saw the field agent, she didn't ask about her pension or relief. She was blessed enough to know where her next meal was coming from.

And unlike many of the other interviewees, Grandmama was faced not with a condescending white woman who wanted to talk about what similarities her former Missus had to Scarlett O'Hara from that book everybody and their mama was talking about, but with a Black interviewer who wanted to hear her real story. He walked in with his pretty young daughter trailing behind him, her own notepad in hand.

Grandmama was also unlike other interviewees in that she'd never considered the mention of her enslavement inappropriate. She remembered wondering about her mother's mother's story, and if it were up to her, none of her grandchildren would ever know such curiosity. She would tell her story as often as she could with as many details as she could remember to keep from creating more Lost Ones in her wake.

"And why should I be ashamed of it, anyway?" she often said. "I surely didn't enslave myself."

She introduced herself in her Mississippi drawl, telling the young man that she'd been born in the Mississippi Delta and lived near about there all her life after slavery.

"My husband and I had three sons together," she said with a twinkle in her eye. "After freedom, we bought a small farm at a fair price, and we worked it together. Did the boys ever work? Only when they weren't in school! Wasn't no way I'd let my boys miss out on an education when I'd sacrificed so much to have one myself."

When he asked her about the sacrifice, Grandmama cringed a bit. She reached up and touched her head where one long, thick braid twirled like a crown around her temples. She told him how Missus had whipped her and shorn her head, how she'd never worn her hair long again in slavery times. Then she told him about how she'd never cut it again once freedom came.

"Except for a little trim on the ends every now and then. I use Annie Turnbo Malone's Poro products," she said, puffing out her chest with pride in "the race."

"Religiously," Granddaughter put in, smiling. It had been a line item in their budget since Grandmama came to live with them. "Though I'm more partial to Madam C. J. myself."

"But she went to Port College up north," Grandmama said, beaming at the younger woman beside her, "and that's how she learned to do hair so fine."

"That's right," Granddaughter said, nodding her head indulgently. "Grandmama talked my parents into letting me go. Said she remembered a day when no one would dream of a Black woman founding an entire hair college and product line, and that I owed it to the race to continue that legacy."

Grandmama nodded emphatically. "Sure did."

The field agent chuckled. His wife had been to Granddaughter's hair salon on more than one occasion, and his daughter would be sitting in her chair later that week to get her hair pressed straight. He could already smell the distinctive scent of Madam C. J. Walker's Wonderful Hair Grower.

"Tell me about your husband," he said, knowing it was one of Grandmama's favorite topics.

Grandmama beamed. He'd still been sun, moon, and stars to her when he died five years ago. "He was the hardest working man I ever knew," she said. "Beat the sun out of bed every morning. Laid down beside me every single night after we found each other. He'd been on his way to get us when we ran into him on the road after emancipation. It was a God thing. He'd joined the Union Army and was unable to get away right after the war. But he found us, and he never let us go again after that."

"And your sons?" he asked.

"I had three of them!" Grandmama said. "And two daughters too. Make sure you write that down. One of my baby girls died as an infant, and the other was sold away. I never did find my little girl, but I like to imagine that she's out there somewhere, doing fine. My sons all grew up to be fine, hardworking men. A teacher, a lawyer, and a doctor."

Granddaughter smiled. She came from the family line of the teacher. He'd headed to DC after graduating from Oberlin College to teach at M Street, the finest Negro school in the country. Her lawyer great-uncle had gone to school in New York, where his family now lived in Brooklyn. Her doctor great-uncle had made his way west with the earliest folks of the Great Migration, and his family was in California now. Her own father had settled back down south in Arkansas, where he'd been an educator like his father until the day he died.

"I've outlived all of my boys," said Grandmama in a subdued tone. "And my husband too."

Granddaughter reached for Grandmama's hand with a reassuring squeeze. The grief of loss had always mingled with the joy of a life well lived despite that loss. Grandmama's hand squeezed back, her grip still strong and sure, and she offered the much younger woman a soft smile.

"But you didn't come here to talk about my progeny," Grandmama said, looking the interviewer straight in the face. "You came here to talk about slavery times. You don't need to beat around the bush. I don't mind sharing."

And for the next two hours, she did.

Grandmama shared about being separated from her mother, about coming to live with her new Missus and taking care of young

Missy. She described how she'd learned to read by listening in on young Missy's lessons, as well as the punishment that ensued when she got caught. She talked about being cast out of the Big House, moving to the slave quarters, and Cook taking her in. And she talked about Sun, about falling in love with him, losing him, having his babies, and living in constant fear that they'd be taken away.

Grandmama reflected on the complexity of her motherhood and her marriage. About not knowing where she came from but trying to take an active role in deciding where she was going. About meeting Jesus in the hollow and crying out to him for justice when she learned how much he hated oppression.

"He heard me," she said. "He freed us. And it sure did seem like he had tarried, but he made his way. And he brought us back together, in the end."

Grandmama talked about Reconstruction too. About how there'd been Black statesmen and how Sun had voted in a few elections before the white folks decided Black folks didn't need to go to the ballot box. She talked about the Klan and how they'd terrorized their small neighborhood of Negro landowners when one of them had dared to try to register to vote.

"They didn't burn crosses in the yards back then," she said. "They didn't start doing that until after *The Birth of a Nation*, you know. What they did do was drag men out of their homes and beat them with whips—if they were lucky. And if they weren't so lucky, you'd find what was left of them scattered all over the woods the next day."

She unveiled this horrific history in such a matter-of-fact way because how else could she tell it? It's what had happened, and it's what was still happening when Black folks down South got out of line.

"I'm praying for the Lord to intervene again. The Bible says he doesn't count time the same way we do. Hundreds of years is the blink of an eye for him." She chuckled. "I'm hoping he blinks again soon and sets things to rights."

At this interview in 1937, she didn't know it but she sat at a period equidistant from slavery's abolition and the election of America's first Black president. But she had spent the balance of her existence living on the steepest slope of that uphill climb. She wouldn't make it to that peak—the one they'd insist was the mountaintop.

Her great-great-great-grandchildren would still be waiting for justice to roll in ways different from the ones she'd pray for. But they'd also achieve strides she could never have imagined as she sat talking about the long road of the life she'd lived so far.

That long road was coming to an end soon. Grandmama knew. "God's going to call me home soon," she told the field agent with a smile. "When I was young, that thought used to terrify me. What if I wasn't ready? What if these young folks are right and there is no heaven and no hell—just an empty space at the end of time? But I've experienced too much of heaven's sweetness here on earth not to trust that there's a fuller version in the hereafter. And I can say the same about hell too."

He asked her about her enslavers—about Marse and Missus and young Missy.

"Last I heard, their people were still in Mississippi," she said. "They're still the wealthy, blue-blooded type. They're Ole Miss people, you know—University of Mississippi, but they call Ole Miss the same way we used to talk about Old Missus. Missus and Marse are long gone, now—and Missy, too, a few years back. But she wrote me a letter once about how much she'd loved playing with me when we were little girls, and how she often thought fondly of those memories together." She sniffed. "I didn't write her back."

"If it'd been up to her mother," Granddaughter put in, "Grandmama wouldn't have even been able to read the letter."

Grandmama chuckled at that. "That much is true. Now, what are you going to do with these interviews?" she asked.

The field agent explained that the Federal Writer's Project was collecting interviews from what they called "ex-slaves" and organizing them all by state.

"Will my interview be in Mississippi or Arkansas?" Grandmama wanted to know.

"Arkansas," said the field worker, "if the editor decides to include it."

"And the editor is a white man?" Grandmama asked ruefully.

"A white woman," said the field agent with a chuckle. "But point taken. She really does want to represent the interviews faithfully, which is more than can be said about some of the other states who have participated. Mississippi has already turned in their interviews—there were less than thirty. Every state has collected at least a few hundred, but Mississippi . . ."

"Mississippi is always going to be Mississippi," Grandmama said in her world-weary way. "And everybody *but* Mississippi knows their dirty laundry stinks too strongly to be hidden."

The man asked a few more questions about the war and Reconstruction and about Grandmama's day-to-day life on the plantation. He asked her about the children's house and about watching her babies at the end of the cotton rows while she worked. He asked about the daughters she had lost, and she told him their stories with the same reverence that always accompanied their telling.

At the end of her interview, Grandmama turned to address the young girl who had been sitting behind her father, scribbling in her own little notebook. "I want to show you something," she said.

Granddaughter was already moving toward the huge cedar chest in the corner, knowing what she wanted to show this young girl. She reached in and started pulling out blankets—quilt after quilt in a riot of colors and textures. She started stacking them on the floor next to the chest, one after another, as Grandmama narrated.

"That's the one I made after I first got to Mississippi."

"That's the one I made after Sun was sold."

"That's the one I made after my daughter was born."

"That's the one I made after emancipation."

Grandmama smiled at the young girl. "All of our stories are in there. All of our history. And all of this is part of your history too, you know."

The young girl nodded, all reverence.

"I'm not your grandmama, but your grandmama was probably somebody like me. And her stories aren't exactly the same as mine, but all of our stories work together to tell you something about our history—Negro history. It's truly a sight to behold. It's truly something to be proud of."

"Yes, ma'am," said the girl, smiling at the attention.

"You'll be part of our history too," said Grandmama. "Go out there and make us proud."

"Yes, ma'am," she replied.

Soon, they wrapped up. The field agent and his daughter made their way toward the front door, wishing Grandmama well as Granddaughter saw them out. Grandmama waved, turning her attention back to the letter in her hand. She picked up the magnifying glass from the side table and tried her best to make out the news from one of her many great-great-grandchildren. All of that talking about the past had kindled her excitement to read more about her future.

NOTES

Introduction

1. Alexis Wells-Oghoghomeh, *The Souls of Womenfolk: The Religious Cultures of Enslaved Women in the Lower South* (Chapel Hill: University of North Carolina Press, 2021), 10.

2. Wells-Oghoghomeh, *Souls of Womenfolk*, 10. Emphasis added.

3. As a nod to my favorite Langston Hughes poem, "Song," which begins, "Lovely, dark, and lonely one."

Chapter 1 Little Bit

1. Jasper Battle, *Slave Narratives*, vol. 4, part 1. In citing the WPA Narratives in these notes, the series will be identified as *Slave Narratives*, plus the name of the person being interviewed and volume number. For complete ebook series information, see Work Projects Administration, *Slave Narratives: A Folk History of Slavery in the United States from Interviews with Former Slaves*, 17 volumes, Project Gutenberg, February 1, 2004, to May 4, 2011, https://www.gutenberg.org/ebooks/author/3906.

2. Squires Jackson, *Slave Narratives*, vol. 3.

3. Charlie Barbour, *Slave Narratives*, vol. 11, part 1.

4. Henry Bland, *Slave Narratives*, vol. 4, part 1.

5. Jessie Rowell, *Slave Narratives*, vol. 3.

6. Elvira Boles, *Slave Narratives*, vol. 16, part 1.

7. Duncan Gaines, *Slave Narratives*, vol. 3.

8. Randall Lee, *Slave Narratives*, vol. 3.

9. Sylvia Lee, *Slave Narratives*, vol. 15.

10. Adeline Hodges, *Slave Narratives*, vol. 1.

11. Oliver Bell, *Slave Narratives*, vol. 1.

12. Frank Bates, *Slave Narratives*, vol. 3.

13. Tom Bates, *Slave Narratives*, vol. 9.

14. Mattie Fannen, *Slave Narratives*, vol. 2, part 2.

15. William Wells Brown, *Narrative of William W. Brown, A Fugitive Slave* (Boston: The Anti-Slavery Office, 1847), 15, https://docsouth.unc.edu/neh/brown47/brown47.html.

16. Norman Burkes, *Slave Narratives*, vol. 2, part 1.

17. John W. H. Barnett, *Slave Narratives*, vol. 2, part 1.

18. Salena Taswell, *Slave Narratives*, vol. 2, part 1.

19. Katherine Clay, *Slave Narratives*, vol. 2, part 2.

20. George P. Rawick, Jan Hillegas, and Ken Lawrence, eds., *Mississippi Narratives Part 4*, supplement series 1, vol. 9 of *The American Slave: A Composite Autobiography* (Westport, CT: Greenwood, 1978), 1629–35. Henry was often whipped for running out looking for his mother.

21. Duncan Gaines, *Slave Narratives*, vol. 3.

22. Madeo Admin, "Black Families Severed by Slavery," Equal Justice Initiative, January 29, 2018, https://eji.org/news/history-racial-injustice-black-families-severed-by-slavery/.

23. Charlie Barbour, *Slave Narratives*, vol. 11, part 1.

24. Viney Baker, *Slave Narratives*, vol. 11, part 1.

25. Laura Clark, *Slave Narratives*, vol. 1.

26. Henry H. Buttler, *Slave Narratives*, vol. 16, part 1.

27. Andy Anderson, *Slave Narratives*, vol. 16, part 1.

28. Sterlin Arwine, *Slave Narratives*, vol. 16, part 1.

29. Josie Brown, *Slave Narratives*, vol. 16, part 1.

30. Sarah Gudger, *Slave Narratives*, vol. 11, part 1.

31. George P. Rawick, Jan Hillegas, and Ken Lawrence, eds., *Texas Narratives Part 10*, supplement series 2, vol. 9 of *The American Slave: A Composite Autobiography* (Westport, CT: Greenwood, 1978), 4110.

32. Millie Williams, *Slave Narratives*, vol. 16, part 4.

33. "WPA Interview with Harriet Hill," *Last Seen: Finding Family after Slavery*, accessed January 22, 2024, https://informationwanted.org/items/show/4772.

34. Frederick Douglass, *My Bondage & My Freedom* (New York: Miller, Orton & Mulligan, 1855), 56, https://docsouth.unc.edu/neh/douglass55/douglass55.html.

35. Frankie Goole, *Slave Narratives*, vol. 15.

36. George P. Rawick, Jan Hillegas, and Ken Lawrence, eds., *Mississippi Narratives Part 1*, supplement series 1, vol. 6 of *The American Slave: A Composite Autobiography* (Westport, CT: Greenwood, 1978), 95.

Chapter 2 Lonely One

1. David Pilgrim, "The Picaninny Caricature," Jim Crow Museum (Big Rapids, MI: Ferris State University, 2000), https://jimcrowmuseum.ferris.edu/antiblack/picaninny/homepage.htm.

2. Carey Davenport, *Slave Narratives*, vol. 16, part 1.

3. Delia Garlic, *Slave Narratives*, vol. 1.

4. Unnamed Informant, *Slave Narratives*, vol. 4, part 4.

5. Mary Armstrong, *Slave Narratives*, vol. 16, part 1.

6. Charles Davenport, *Slave Narratives*, vol. 9.

7. Jeptha Choice, *Slave Narratives*, vol. 16, part 1.

8. Clayborn Gantling, *Slave Narratives*, vol. 3.

9. Callie Williams, *Slave Narratives*, vol. 1.

10. Sam and Louisa Everett, *Slave Narratives*, vol. 3.

11. Betty Curlett, *Slave Narratives*, vol. 2, part 2.

12. Katie Darling, *Slave Narratives*, vol. 16, part 1.

13. George Womble, *Slave Narratives*, vol. 4, part 4.

14. Mose Banks, *Slave Narratives*, vol. 2, part 1.

15. Sarah Gudger, *Slave Narratives*, vol. 11, part 1.

16. Mariah Hines, *Slave Narratives*, vol. 17.

17. Robert Falls, *Slave Narratives*, vol. 15.

18. Charles L. Perdue Jr., Thomas E. Barden, and Robert K. Phillips, eds., *Weevils in the Wheat: Interviews with Virginia Ex-Slaves* (Charlottesville: University of Virginia Press, 1976), 191.

19. Kendra Hamilton, "*Negro in Virginia, The* (1940)," Encyclopedia Virginia, August 30, 2021, https://encyclopediavirginia.org/entries/negro-in-virginia-the-1940/. See also Catherine A. Stewart, *Long Past Slavery: Representing Race in the Federal Writers' Project* (Chapel Hill: University of North Carolina Press, 2016).

20. Monroe Brackins, *Slave Narratives*, vol. 16, part 1.

21. Mary Ella Grandberry, *Slave Narratives*, vol. 1.

22. Louisa Adams, *Slave Narratives*, vol. 11, part 1.

23. Dora Franks, *Slave Narratives*, vol. 9.

24. Adeline Blakely, *Slave Narratives*, vol. 2, part 1.

25. James Singleton, *Slave Narratives*, vol. 9.

26. John W. Blassingame, *Slave Testimony* (Baton Rouge: Louisiana State University Press, 1977), 46–47.

27. Blassingame, *Slave Testimony*, 96.

28. Blassingame, *Slave Testimony*, 95.

29. Blassingame, *Slave Testimony*, 108.

30. Sallie Crane, *Slave Narratives*, vol. 2, part 2.

Interlude: Cornelia

1. Cornelia Andrews, *Slave Narratives*, vol. 11, part 1.

2. The first Black student had been admitted in 1870, but Jeremiah Armstrong was the first Black graduate, in 1910.

Chapter 3 Lovely

1. George P. Rawick, Jan Hillegas, and Ken Lawrence, eds., *The Unwritten History of Slavery*, vol. 18 of *The American Slave: A Composite Autobiography* (Westport, CT: Greenwood, 1978), 34.

2. Rawick, Hillegas, and Lawrence, *Unwritten History of Slavery*, 8.

3. Elvira Boles, *Slave Narratives*, vol. 16, part 1.

4. John C. Bectom, *Slave Narratives*, vol. 11, part 1.

5. Rawick, Hillegas, and Lawrence, *Unwritten History of Slavery*, 8.

6. Analiza Foster, *Slave Narratives*, vol. 11, part 1.

7. John Henry Kemp, *Slave Narratives*, vol. 3.

8. Rawick, Hillegas, and Lawrence, *Unwritten History of Slavery*, 5.

9. Homer, *The Iliad*, trans. Alexander Pope (1899; Project Gutenberg, 2002), bk. 6, https://www.gutenberg.org/files/6130/6130-h/6130-h.htm.

10. Julia Brown, *Slave Narratives*, vol. 4, part 1.

11. Elizabeth Sparks, *Slave Narratives*, vol. 17.

12. James Calhart, *Slave Narratives*, vol. 8.

13. John Walton, *Slave Narratives*, vol. 16, part 4.

14. Rawick, Hillegas, and Lawrence, *Mississippi Narratives Part 1*, 217–18.

15. Sallie Crane, *Slave Narratives*, vol. 2, part 2.

16. Julia Blanks, *Slave Narratives*, vol. 16, part 1.

17. Louis Cain, *Slave Narratives*, vol. 16, part 1.

18. Elizabeth Sparks, *Slave Narratives*, vol. 17.

19. Sam and Louisa Everett, *Slave Narratives*, vol. 3.
20. Elige Davison, *Slave Narratives*, vol. 16, part 1.
21. Jeptha Choice, *Slave Narratives*, vol. 16, part 1.
22. Sam and Louisa Everett, *Slave Narratives*, vol. 3.
23. Sam and Louisa Everett, *Slave Narratives*, vol. 3.
24. Kimberly C. Moore, "Mulberry Couple Told of Horrific Life as Slaves," *The Ledger*, September 14, 2020, https://www.theledger.com/story/news/2020/09/14/black-polk-mulberry-couple-told-horrific-life-slaves/3340392001/.
25. John Barker, *Slave Narratives*, vol. 16, part 1.
26. Tom Douglas, *Slave Narratives*, vol. 2, part 2.
27. Jim Allen, *Slave Narratives*, vol. 9.
28. Josephine Anderson, *Slave Narratives*, vol. 3.
29. Georgina Giwbs, *Slave Narratives*, vol. 17.
30. Will Glass, *Slave Narratives*, vol. 2, part 3.
31. Sylvia Watkins, *Slave Narratives*, vol. 15.
32. Ambrose Douglass, *Slave Narratives*, vol. 3.
33. Arnold Gragston, *Slave Narratives*, vol. 3.
34. Lowcountry Digital History Initiative, "Escaping Slavery," *Hidden Voices: Enslaved Women in the Lowcountry and U.S. South* (exhibit), College of Charleston, accessed September 10, 2023, https://ldhi.library.cofc.edu/exhibits/show/hidden-voices/resisting-enslavement/escaping-slavery.

Chapter 4 Cherished

1. Jeptha Choice, *Slave Narratives*, vol. 16, part 1.
2. Minnie Fulkes, *Slave Narratives*, vol. 17.
3. John W. Blassingame, *The Slave Community: Plantation Life in the Antebellum South*, rev. and enlarged ed. (New York: Oxford University Press, 1979), 164.
4. Bethany Veney, *The Narrative of Bethany Veney, A Slave Woman* (Worcester, MA, 1889), 18, https://docsouth.unc.edu/fpn/veney/veney.html.
5. Charles Ball, *Slavery in the United States: A Narrative of the Life and Adventures of Charles Ball, a Black Man, Who Lived Forty Years in Maryland, South Carolina and Georgia, as a Slave under Various Masters, and Was One Year in the Navy with Commodore Barney, during the Late War* (New York: John S. Taylor, 1837), 37, https://docsouth.unc.edu/neh/ballslavery/ball.html.
6. Veney, *Narrative of Bethany Veney*, 20.
7. Mattie Fannen, *Slave Narratives*, vol. 2, part 2.
8. Malindy Maxwell, *Slave Narratives*, vol. 2, part 5.
9. Jim Allen, *Slave Narratives*, vol. 9.
10. Sarah Debro, "Slave Narrative of Sarah Debro," Access Genealogy, August 12, 2012, https://accessgenealogy.com/north-carolina/slave-narrative-of-sarah-debro.htm.
11. Henry Doyl, *Slave Narratives*, vol. 2, part 2.
12. Benjamin Drew, *The Refugee: Or the Narratives of Fugitive Slaves in Canada. Related by Themselves, with an Account of the History and Condition of the Colored Population of Upper Canada* (Boston: John P Jewett and Company, 1856), 29, https://docsouth.unc.edu/neh/drew/drew.html.
13. W. L. Bost, *Slave Narratives*, vol. 11, part 1.
14. Rachel Adams, *Slave Narratives*, vol. 4, part 1.
15. J. H. Beckwith, *Slave Narratives*, vol. 2, part 1.
16. Susan Snow, *Slave Narratives*, vol. 9.

17. Jasper Battle, *Slave Narratives*, vol. 4, part 1.

18. John Anderson, *The Story of the Life of John Anderson, the Fugitive Slave* (London: William Tweedie, 1863), 125, https://docsouth.unc.edu/neh/twelvetr/twelvetr.html.

19. Henry Bibb, *Narrative of the Life and Adventures of Henry Bibb, An American Slave, Written by Himself* (New York, 1849), 42, https://docsouth.unc.edu/neh/bibb/bibb.html.

20. Moses Grandy, *Narrative of the Life of Moses Grandy; Late a Slave in the United States of America* (London: C. Gilpin, 1843), 25, https://docsouth.unc.edu/fpn/grandy/grandy.html.

21. Ned Sublette and Constance Sublette, *American Slave Coast: A History of the Slave-Breeding Industry* (Chicago: Chicago Review, 2017), 80.

22. James Martin, *Slave Narratives*, vol. 16, part 3.

23. Callie Williams, *Slave Narratives*, vol. 1.

24. Della Harris, *Slave Narratives*, vol. 17.

25. Mary James, *Slave Narratives*, vol. 8.

26. Rose Williams, *Slave Narratives*, vol. 16, part 4.

27. Anne Clark, *Slave Narratives*, vol. 16, part 1.

28. Ronnie W. Clayton, *Mother Wit: The Ex-Slave Narratives of the Louisiana Writers' Project* (New York: Peter Lang, 1990), 66.

29. Mandy McCullough Crosby, *Slave Narratives*, vol. 1.

30. Jennifer L. Morgan, "*Partus Sequitur Ventrem*: Law, Race, and Reproduction in Colonial Slavery," *Columbia Law School* (blog), accessed September 11, 2023, https://blogs.law.columbia.edu/abolition1313/files/2020/08/Morgan-Partus-1.pdf.

31. Tempie Herdon Durham, *Slave Narratives*, vol. 11, part 1.

32. Maggie (Bunny) Bond, *Slave Narratives*, vol. 2, part 1.

Interlude: Mary

1. Clayton, *Mother Wit*, 94–95.

Chapter 5 Mother

1. Easter Sudie Campbell, *Slave Narratives*, vol. 7.

2. Della Briscoe, *Slave Narratives*, vol. 4, part 1.

3. Annie Bridges, *Slave Narratives*, vol. 10.

4. Josephine Smith, *Slave Narratives*, vol. 11, part 2.

5. Roberta Manson, *Slave Narratives*, vol. 11, part 2.

6. Mrs. Rhuben Gilbert, *Slave Narratives*, vol. 7.

7. Nancy Boudry, *Slave Narratives*, vol. 4, part 1.

8. Julia Brown, *Slave Narratives*, vol. 4, part 1.

9. George P. Rawick, Jan Hillegas, and Ken Lawrence, eds., *Mississippi Narratives Part* 2, supplement series 1, vol. 7 of *The American Slave: A Composite Autobiography* (Westport, CT: Greenwood, 1978), 379–85.

10. Rawick, Hillegas, and Lawrence, *Mississippi Narratives Part 1*, 308–12.

11. Veney, *Narrative of Bethany Veney*, 26.

12. Celia Robinson, *Slave Narratives*, vol. 11, part 2.

13. Jennifer L. Morgan, *Laboring Women: Reproduction and Gender in New World Slavery* (Philadelphia: University of Pennsylvania Press, 2004), 166.

14. John Brown, *Slave Life in Georgia: A Narrative of the Life, Sufferings, and Escape of John Brown, a Fugitive Slave, Now in England* (London, 1855), 3–4, https://docsouth.unc.edu/neh/jbrown/jbrown.html.

15. Louis Hamilton, *Slave Narratives*, vol. 10.
16. Becky Hawkins, *Slave Narratives*, vol. 2, part 3.
17. Rawick, Hillegas, and Lawrence, *Texas Narratives Part 10*, 4110.
18. Cheney Cross, *Slave Narratives*, vol. 1.
19. Jeptha Choice, *Slave Narratives*, vol. 16, part 1.
20. Charlotte Beverly, *Slave Narratives*, vol. 16, part 1.
21. Ank Bishop, *Slave Narratives*, vol. 1.
22. Clayton, *Mother Wit*, 65.
23. Henry Doyl Brinkly, *Slave Narratives*, vol. 2, part 2.
24. Ida Blackshear Hutchinson, *Slave Narratives*, vol. 2, part 3.
25. Elvira Boles, *Slave Narratives*, vol. 16, part 1.

Chapter 6 Lost One

1. "Value of Negro Property," *Hinds County Gazette*, September 14, 1862.
2. Stewart, *Long Past Slavery*, 180.
3. Samuel Simeon Andrews, *Slave Narratives*, vol. 3.
4. Molly Reid Cleaver, "'Lost Friends' Ads Reveal the Heartbreak of Family Separation during Slavery," The Historic New Orleans Collection, November 27, 2018, https://www.hnoc.org/publications/first-draft/lost-friends-ads-reveal-heartbreak-family-separation-during-slavery.
5. "Lost Friends: Advertisements from the *Southwestern Christian Advocate*," The Historic New Orleans Collection, accessed December 19, 2023, https://www.hnoc.org/database/lost-friends/index.html.
6. Robert Glenn, *Slave Narratives*, vol. 11, part 1.
7. Lizzie Baker, *Slave Narratives*, vol. 11, part 1.
8. Tinie Force and Elvira Lewis, *Slave Narratives*, vol. 7.
9. Jennie Davis, *Slave Narratives*, vol. 2, part 2.
10. Norman Burkes, *Slave Narratives*, vol. 2, part 1.
11. Ellaine Wright, *Slave Narratives*, vol. 10.
12. Cora L. Horton, *Slave Narratives*, vol. 2, part 3.
13. Augustus Ladson, *Slave Narratives*, vol. 14, part 1.
14. Clayton, *Mother Wit*, 20–23.
15. Unnamed Informant, *Slave Narratives*, vol. 14, part 1.
16. Hannah Crasson, *Slave Narratives*, vol. 11, part 1.
17. Mary Gaines, *Slave Narratives*, vol. 2, part 3.

Interlude: Elizabeth

1. Elizabeth Sparks, *Slave Narratives*, vol. 17.

Chapter 7 Sister

1. Jacob Branch, *Slave Narratives*, vol. 16, part 1.
2. Charlie Van Dyke, *Slave Narratives*, vol. 1.
3. Clayborn Gantling, *Slave Narratives*, vol. 3.
4. Louisa Adams, *Slave Narratives*, vol. 11, part 1.
5. Charity Austin, *Slave Narratives*, vol. 11, part 1.
6. Millie Simpkins, *Slave Narratives*, vol. 15.
7. Laura Abromson, *Slave Narratives*, vol. 2, part 1.
8. Chaney Hews, *Slave Narratives*, vol. 11, part 1.
9. Ellen Claiborne, *Slave Narratives*, vol. 4, part 1.

10. Robert Hinton, *Slave Narratives*, vol. 11, part 1.
11. Ellen Betts, *Slave Narratives*, vol. 16, part 1.
12. Marthala Grant, *Slave Narratives*, vol. 2, part 3.
13. Anthony Abercrombie, *Slave Narratives*, vol. 1.
14. Mary Anderson, *Slave Narratives*, vol. 11, part 1.
15. Rachel Adams, *Slave Narratives*, vol. 4.
16. Mack Mullen, *Slave Narratives*, vol. 3.
17. Jane Arrington, *Slave Narratives*, vol. 11, part 1.
18. Lucretia Alexander, *Slave Narratives*, vol. 2, part 1.
19. Celestia Avery, *Slave Narratives*, vol. 4, part 1.
20. W. B. Allen, *Slave Narratives*, vol. 4, part 1.
21. William M. Adams, *Slave Narratives*, vol. 16, part 1.
22. Mary Colbert, *Slave Narratives*, vol. 4, part 1.
23. Hannah Crasson, *Slave Narratives*, vol. 11, part 1.
24. Julia Blanks, *Slave Narratives*, vol. 16, part 1.
25. Robert Falls, *Slave Narratives*, vol. 15.
26. Annie Hawkins, *Slave Narratives*, vol. 13.
27. Randall Lee, *Slave Narratives*, vol. 3.
28. Blassingame, *Slave Testimony*, 276–84.

Chapter 8 Dove

1. "The Lincoln Proclamation," *Natchez Daily Courier*, January 9, 1863, 1.
2. "Telegraphic News Reported Expressly to the Courier," *Natchez Daily Courier*, January 13, 1863.
3. Minnie Davis, *Slave Narratives*, vol. 4, part 1.
4. Victoria McMullen, *Slave Narratives*, vol. 2, part 5.
5. Alice Douglass, *Slave Narratives*, vol. 13.
6. Squires Jackson, *Slave Narratives*, vol. 3.
7. Elvira Boles, *Slave Narratives*, vol. 16, part 1.
8. Fred Brown, *Slave Narratives*, vol. 16, part 1.
9. Wash Ingram, *Slave Narratives*, vol. 16, part 2.
10. Boston Blackwell, *Slave Narratives*, vol. 2, part 1.
11. W. E. B. Du Bois, *Black Reconstruction in America: An Essay toward a History of the Part Which Black Folk Played in the Attempt to Reconstruct Democracy in America, 1860–1880* (New York: Oxford University Press, 2014), Kindle loc. 2696.
12. Louis Lucas, *Slave Narratives*, vol. 2, part 4.
13. U.S. National Park Service, "The Legacy of the Maryland Campaign," Born of Earnest Struggle Series, National Park Service, last updated August 14, 2017, https://www.nps.gov/articles/the-legacy-of-the-maryland-campaign.htm.
14. U.S. National Park Service, "Legacy of the Maryland Campaign."
15. Carey Davenport, *Slave Narratives*, vol. 16, part 1.
16. Laura Cornish, *Slave Narratives*, vol. 16, part 1.
17. Felix Haywood, *Slave Narratives*, vol. 16, part 1.
18. Malindy Maxwell, *Slave Narratives*, vol. 2, part 5.
19. Reginald Washington, "Sealing the Sacred Bonds of Holy Matrimony: Freedmen's Bureau Marriage Records," *Genealogy Notes* 37, no. 1 (Spring 2005), https://www.archives.gov/publications/prologue/2005/spring/freedman-marriage-recs.html.
20. "Alexander Foley and His Wife Reunited and Remarried after Forty Years," *The Evening Bulletin* (Maysville, KY), November 27, 1891, https://informationwanted.org/items/show/3289.

21. "Jeff Frierson and Mary Burt Reunited and Remarried after 44-Year Separation," *The Nashville (TN) American*, September 25, 1903, https://informationwanted.org/items/show/3568.

22. "Solomon Terry Never Reunited with Family," *Minneapolis (MN) Journal*, February 11, 1903, https://informationwanted.org/items/show/2861.

23. "George Reed Searching for His Daughter Kittie," *Southwestern Christian Advocate* (New Orleans, LA), June 3, 1880, https://informationwanted.org/items/show/4660.

24. "Mrs. Anna Mollie Wright Reunited with Her Daughter Mrs. Anna Freeman after 29 Years," *The Wheeling (WV) Daily Intelligencer*, April 11, 1892, https://informationwanted.org/items/show/3261.

25. "Hiram Jefferson Reunited with Son Thomas after 30 Years," *Daily State Gazette* (Green Bay, WI), November 15, 1893, https://informationwanted.org/items/show/3254.

26. "Unidentified Parents Reunited with Their Daughter after 20 Years," *Baltimore Sun*, July 29, 1875, https://informationwanted.org/items/show/3236.

27. Sarah Frances Shaw Graves (Aunt Sally), *Slave Narratives*, vol. 10.

28. Virginia Bell, *Slave Narratives*, vol. 16, part 1.

29. Hannah Rosen, *Terror in the Heart of Freedom: Citizenship, Sexual Violence, and the Meaning of Race in the Postemancipation South* (Chapel Hill: University of North Carolina Press, 2009), 10.

30. Herbert G. Gutman, *The Black Family in Slavery and Freedom: 1750–1925* (New York: Vintage Books, 1977), 6–7.

31. "Alexander Foley and His Wife Reunited."

32. "Milton Douglas Reuniting with His Wife," *Southwestern Christian Advocate* (New Orleans, LA), September 7, 1882, https://informationwanted.org/items/show/4520.

Interlude: Samuel Shinkle Taylor

1. Linda Lovell, "Samuel Shinkle Taylor (1886–1956)," Encyclopedia of Arkansas, accessed June 16, 2023, https://encyclopediaofarkansas.net/entries/samuel-shinkle-taylor-4030/.

2. Zora Neale Hurston, *Mules and Men* (New York: Amistad, 2008), 2–3.

3. Lucretia Alexander, *Slave Narratives*, vol. 2, part 1.

4. J. F. Boone, *Slave Narratives*, vol. 2, part 1.

5. W. A. Anderson, *Slave Narratives*, vol. 2, part 1.

6. Ellen Cragin, *Slave Narratives*, vol. 2, part 2.

7. Fannie Dorum, *Slave Narratives*, vol. 2, part 2.

8. Waters McIntosh, *Slave Narratives*, vol. 2, part 5.

9. Amanda Ross, *Slave Narratives*, vol. 2, part 6.

10. Martha Ruffin, *Slave Narratives*, vol. 2, part 6.

11. Betty Johnson, *Slave Narratives*, vol. 2, part 4.

12. There is one other interviewer in Arkansas whose thoroughness stands out: Miss Irene Robertson. She has not Taylor's compassion but does echo his thoroughness.

13. Lovell, "Samuel Shinkle Taylor."

14. Lovell, "Samuel Shinkle Taylor." Now, the particulars of the comment vetting process of the Encyclopedia of Arkansas are unknown to the writer. But they do require both an email and phone number from the commenter in their vetting process, and the full name of Taylor's daughter is given.

15. Gus Brown, *Slave Narratives*, vol. 1.

16. Simon Phillips, *Slave Narratives*, vol. 1.

17. Sallie Crane, *Slave Narratives*, vol. 2, part 2.

Jasmine L. Holmes

is a passionate writer and educator who celebrates Black stories through her books and public history resources. With a love for literature and academic rigor, she immerses herself in research to uncover the hidden narratives that shape our world. Her commitment to centering Black experiences shines through in her writing, which includes the books *Carved in Ebony*, *Mother to Son*, and *Crowned with Glory*. As a research assistant and teacher, Jasmine shares her expertise with lifelong learners and educators alike, inspiring them to expand their understanding of history and its impact on our society. Alongside her husband and three sons, Jasmine calls Jackson, Mississippi, home.

CONNECT WITH JASMINE:

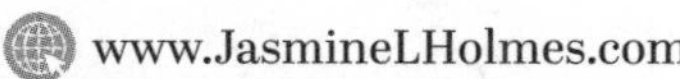

www.JasmineLHolmes.com

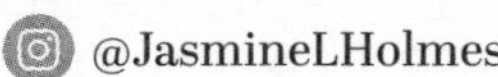

@JasmineLHolmes